A Vampire Reflects

by

Frank Semerano

New York Hollywood London Toronto

SAMUELFRENCH.COM

Copyright © 2008 by Frank Semerano
ALL RIGHTS RESERVED

CAUTION: Professionals and amateurs are hereby warned that *A VAMPIRE REFLECTS* is subject to a royalty. It is fully protected under the copyright laws of the United States of America, the British Commonwealth, including Canada, and all other countries of the Copyright Union. All rights, including professional, amateur, motion picture, recitation, lecturing, public reading, radio broadcasting, television and the rights of translation into foreign languages are strictly reserved. In its present form the play is dedicated to the reading public only.

The amateur live stage performance rights to *A VAMPIRE REFLECTS* are controlled exclusively by Samuel French, Inc., and royalty arrangements and licenses must be secured well in advance of presentation. PLEASE NOTE that amateur royalty fees are set upon application in accordance with your producing circumstances. When applying for a royalty quotation and license please give us the number of performances intended, dates of production, your seating capacity and admission fee. Royalties are payable one week before the opening performance of the play to Samuel French, Inc., at 45 W. 25th Street, New York, NY 10010.

Royalty of the required amount must be paid whether the play is presented for charity or gain and whether or not admission is charged.

Stock royalty quoted upon application to Samuel French, Inc.

For all other rights than those stipulated above, apply to: Samuel French, Inc., at 45 W. 25th Street, New York, NY 10010.

Particular emphasis is laid on the question of amateur or professional readings, permission and terms for which must be secured in writing from Samuel French, Inc.

Copying from this book in whole or in part is strictly forbidden by law, and the right of performance is not transferable.

Whenever the play is produced the following notice must appear on all programs, printing and advertising for the play: "Produced by special arrangement with Samuel French, Inc."

Due authorship credit must be given on all programs, printing and advertising for the play.

ISBN 978-0-573-66294-2   Printed in U.S.A.   #24649

No one shall commit or authorize any act or omission by which the copyright of, or the right to copyright, this play may be impaired.

No one shall make any changes in this play for the purpose of production.

Publication of this play does not imply availability for performance. Both amateurs and professionals considering a production are strongly advised in their own interests to apply to Samuel French, Inc., for written permission before starting rehearsals, advertising, or booking a theatre.

No part of this book may be reproduced, stored in a retrieval system, or transmitted in any form, by any means, now known or yet to be invented, including mechanical, electronic, photocopying, recording, videotaping, or otherwise, without the prior written permission of the publisher.

IMPORTANT BILLING AND CREDIT REQUIREMENTS

All producers of *A VAMPIRE REFLECTS* must give credit to the Author of the Play in all programs distributed in connection with performances of the Play, and in all instances in which the title of the Play appears for the purposes of advertising, publicizing or otherwise exploiting the Play and/or a production. The name of the Author *must* appear on a separate line on which no other name appears, immediately following the title and *must* appear in size of type not less than fifty percent of the size of the title type.

CHARACTERS

COLONEL JOHN PUDDLEPONT: In command of a small army outpost in the middle of the southwestern desert.

MRS. LENORA PUDDLEPONT: John's wife.

LT. CRISIS: The major's subordinate, in charge of a loosely classified experiment involving bats.

DR. WOLFBAINE GUNTER: A captured German scientist lending his expertise to the experiment.

JOYCE LYONHARTT: A young lady

COUNT ZESCU: A Vampire visiting the American Southwest for his health.

MATTIE: A female student, infatuated with Count Zescu and protecting him.

SCENE

A long abandoned estate in the middle of the desert, and adjacent to an army post in Heatstroke, California.

TIME

The 1950's just before Valentine's Day.

A VAMPIRE REFLECTS was first presented by Gary Savona at the Ventura Court Theater in Studio City, California on September 23, 1999. The play was produced by Vaughn Armstrong and Gary Savona; directed by Vaughn Armstrong; music by Gary Stockdale; staged managed by Jonathan Simper-Turney; lighting design by Nathan Sykes; costumes by Kristine Wright; set design by Ivonski; sound effects by Jonathan Simper-Turney and Gary Savona; set construction/special effects by Jaymes Wheeler; poster design by Mary Gallien. The cast was as follows:

```
COUNT ZESCU ............................. Anthony De Longis
COLONEL PUDDLEPONT ........................... Dan Payne
MRS. LENORE PUDDLEPONT ....................... Joy Ellison
MATTIE ........................................... Cassie Fox
DR. GUNTER ................................. Miguel Marcott
LIEUTENANT CRISIS ............................... Alex Cobo
JOYCE LYONHARTT ............................... Chris Edsey
```

For Iris Huerta

ACT 1

Scene 1

SETTING: *The main living room of an abandoned estate just recently occupied.*

AT RISE: *The room is empty. The LIGHTS quickly STROBE ON and OFF in synchronization to the SOUND of loud thunder claps for a few seconds until BLACKOUT. After a moment, the LIGHTS SLOWLY FADE UP, and a voice with a thick Eastern European accent can be heard gravely intoning the following words from OFFSTAGE, though the words echo throughout the room.*

OFFSTAGE. In the years following World War II, the United States Army embarked on an experimental project it was hoped would change the course of modern warfare. The project was terminated shortly after it began. No published version of The Congressional Record of the time uses the word Vampire in accounting for the project's abrupt cancellation. Therefore any resemblance to persons living, dead or *undead* is purely coincidental. Though sometimes, come to think of it...I *just* wonder.

*(As the LIGHTS come up FULL, A young lady, **JOYCE LYONHARTT**, wearing an apron and carrying a feather duster enters from upstairs. She looks around to make sure no one is watching and quickly goes to a locked door leading to the cellar and tries to open it. **MATTIE**, a young student, enters through the front door. Shs is wearing a poodle skirt, and has a ponytail. Shs sees **JOYCE** trying to open the locked cellar door)*

MATTIE. What are you doing? I told you to stay out of the cellar!

JOYCE. Just trying to do my job.

MATTIE. There's dust on the floor. I call that sloppy.

JOYCE. It used to be on the furniture. I call that progress.

(**JOYCE** *removes a flask from her pocket and drinks.*)

MATTIE. You know, for a cleaning lady…

JOYCE. Maintenance engineer. It's the 1950's, Dearie. Today a young, sexually-exciting, good-looking woman can grow up to be anything she wants.

MATTIE. Like I said, for a cleaning lady you leave a lot to be desired. I can't continue living in a place like this.

JOYCE. Gee, tough break for the neighbors.

MATTIE. The point is the owner is not supposed to know anyone is helping me keep house.

JOYCE. Well, then I think I've done a pretty good job.

(**JOYCE** *takes another drink.*)

Who, uh…is the owner anyway?

MATTIE. Let's just say it would be wise if you weren't here when he arrived. He doesn't possess my patience.

JOYCE. Well, don't let him steal your personality either.

MATTIE. Look, we made an agreement. You are to leave an hour before the sunsets. It's almost dark.

JOYCE. But I'm not done.

(*A clock starts striking off the hours.*)

MATTIE. You're done, you're done. Here's your money. Now go.

(**MATTIE** *opens the door, but* **JOYCE** *pauses.*)

JOYCE. But I don't feel right leaving the house before I've finished cleaning it. I mean would you go out and meet people before you finished making yourself look presentable…

(**JOYCE** *looks closely at* **MATTIE.**)

JOYCE *(Continued)* Sorry, bad example.

MATTIE. Oh look, somebody left a full bottle of cheap scotch on the porch.

(**JOYCE** *turns around and* **MATTIE** *shoves her through the door and locks it. The clock stops ringing.* **COUNT ZESCU** *enters through the cellar door. he speaks with a thick eastern European accent, and wears a sash and cape, looking very evil, with a giant spider resting on his shoulder.*)

MATTIE. You look magnificent! All who see you will fear you.

COUNT. They will have good reason to fear.

MATTIE. The malevolent eyebrows…the wicked cape…the spider resting on your shoulder.

COUNT. Yes the spider…SPIDER! Get it off!

(*The* **COUNT** *runs around the room frantically trying to brush the spider off his shoulder, as* **MATTIE** *chases him trying to help.*)

MATTIE. I'm sorry, Count. I had assumed it was one of your familiars – you know. Evil spirits assuming animal form.

COUNT. Is it gone?! Is it gone?! I think I felt it crawl down my back.

MATTIE. No Count, you're fine. It's gone.

COUNT. That was close. Evil spirits assuming animal form, indeed! Poor housekeeping is more like it. What do you do during the day anyway?

MATTIE. I pledged my eternal servitude to you.

COUNT. What, you can't pledge while using a mop and a broom once in a while? Young lady, you try my patience.

MATTIE. Wait a minute. You have a loose thread on your shirt.

(**MATTIE** *pulls the thread and the front of the shirt immediately rolls up like a window shade and hits the*

COUNT *in the face.*)

MATTIE *(Continued)* Sorry.

*(The **COUNT**, feeling perspiration on his forehead, tries to remove the handkerchief from his pocket. It doesn't give, until finally, with a firm yank, he pulls it out, tearing a big hole out of his coat.)*

MATTIE *(Continued)* I sewed your handkerchief to your pocket. Remember, it's for show, not for blow.

*(The **COUNT** shakes his head and uses the torn piece of clothing to calmly brush some lint off his sash.)*

MATTIE *(Continued)* All right. I was wrong. But at least we can agree that your sash should hang on the other side.

*(**MATTIE** takes off the Count's sash and his pants fall down.)*

MATTIE *(Continued)* Oh. I didn't know they were holding up your pants. Did I forget to pack your belt again?

COUNT. *(Plaintively)* Why do you wish to serve me?

MATTIE. I love you because you're such a rebel.

*(The **COUNT** begins to dress himself again.)*

COUNT. Rebel? I come from one of the oldest aristocratic and conservative families in Europe. And at one time, one of the best dressed.

MATTIE. No. You're a rebel. Just like James Dean.

*(**MATTIE** takes out a sewing kit, pushes HIM into a chair, and begins mending his pocket)*

MATTIE *(Continued)* It was fate when you called our country and asked for a Foreign Exchange Student.

COUNT. I merely thought I was ordering out a meal. I didn't expect you to move in.

(Pause)

What is that in your pocket?

*(**MATTIE** hands the **COUNT** a card.)*

What is this?

MATTIE. It's for you. Tomorrow is Valentine's Day, my favorite day of the year.

COUNT. Really? You mean that? It is my favorite day also!

MATTIE. To me it is a day unlike any other.

COUNT. Yes. A day where in a small garage in Chicago, eight gangsters were shot on orders from Al Capone. And as their blood freely poured forth from tiny little holes creating a red sea, we give thanks for little favors…

(MATTIE stares at the COUNT. The COUNT opens up the card and looks at it)

Oh. And of course, there is the love too, with the kissing and the hugging and the holding hands…

MATTIE. Didn't you buy me anything?

COUNT. Uhhh…You must wait until tomorrow.

MATTIE. I knew you wouldn't forget.

(She finishes sewing and bites the loose thread with her teeth.)

There! All done.

COUNT. Very nice. But where did you put the needle?

MATTIE. In the pincushion.

COUNT. We don't have a pincushion.

(The COUNT holds up his thumb, showing her the pin sticking out of it.)

MATTIE. Does it hurt?

COUNT. *(Yelling)* OF COURSE IT HURTS!

MATTIE. But you're immortal.

COUNT. And the prospect is beginning to depress me.

(The COUNT removes the needle from his thumb and throws it down.)

I have a headache. I am going to bed early. Where is my coffin?

MATTIE. About that…

COUNT. I am not sleeping in the tanning booth again!

MATTIE. But a coffin would invite suspicion.

COUNT. And a tanning booth in the middle of the desert won't?

MATTIE. This is California, silly.

COUNT. You have defied my will for the last time!

*(The **COUNT** overturns a small table, and **MATTIE** cowers in the corner.)*

COUNT *(Continued)* I shall now turn you into one of the living dead!

MATTIE. Living dead?

(HE moves towards her menacingly.)

COUNT. You leave me no choice. My father was right. There is no room for sentiment in this business. He had armies of the living dead, obeying his every command without question. Come to me, you cannot resist me.

*(**MATTIE** throws herself into the count's arms, and offers her neck to him.)*

MATTIE. Yes, for eternity, I'll be yours. Every moment together. Never apart. Not for an hour. Not for a minute. Not for a second.

COUNT. *(Rethinking the idea)* Hmmmm... .

MATTIE. We'll even visit Mother together.

COUNT. Mother?

MATTIE. You remember Mother.

COUNT. *(Slowly remembering)* Yes...I do. She...met us at the train station?

MATTIE. There was no train.

COUNT. But I distinctly remember seeing a large caboose somewhere. Uh-oh.

MATTIE. Bite me.

*(The **COUNT** tries to extricate himself from **MATTIE**'s passionately entwining embrace, but with no success)*

COUNT. No, no. I believe you have learned your lesson.

MATTIE. Take me. My breasts are soft and milky white.

COUNT. So are mine. The tanning booth shall prove to be quite useful after all. Good move, Mattie.

(He finally pushes her away, and runs behind the table he knocked over, keeping it between him and her.)

MATTIE. *(Hurt)* Then you're not going to turn me into one of the living dead?

COUNT. No, you wouldn't like it. After a while, the living dead tend to flake off a lot on the floor. Father was always complaining about having to follow them around the house with the vacuum cleaner.

MATTIE. You sure are moody tonight. Why don't you turn into a wolf and I'll take you for a walk.

COUNT. I do not want to go for a walk. There's a female Labrador Retriever out there whose mind is not on retrieving sticks, I can tell you that!

MATTIE. Then turn into a cat and you can sit on my lap.

COUNT. Dear child, will you get it through your head that I am a vampire. Not a magician. I cannot turn into a cat. Or pull a rabbit out of my hat. Or make smoke come out of my ears! Oh, excuse me, I was able to make smoke come out of my ears once. When you pulled up the window shades an hour before the sun set! Perhaps you'd like to see me do that again!

*(**MATTIE** starts to sniffle.)*

Or for cryin' out…I am sorry. I will turn into a wolf. But we will play in the backyard. I do not want to be picked up by the pound again, and get another deworming. Now where did you put my ball.

*(**MATTIE** runs to a box and takes out a ball and bounces it up and down.)*

MATTIE. Let's go!

*(The **COUNT** grimaces, strains and squeezes his eyes shut but nothing happens.)*

MATTIE. What happened?

COUNT. It might be easier, if you were not watching.

MATTIE. I understand.

(She turns around. The **COUNT** *grimaces, strains and squeezes his eyes shut but still nothing happens.)*

COUNT. Strange. This has never happened before.

MATTIE. Hmmm…Would it help if I showed you some pictures of Lassie without her collar?

COUNT. It is not that kind of problem! I know. It must have been the long plane flight over the Atlantic. All my internal clocks must be off or something.

MATTIE. That's terrible.

COUNT. Maybe I should have flown in by myself, but would my arms be tired. Which I understand is a big joke in Las Vegas, though the humor of the situation has always escaped me. Well, goodnight.

(The **COUNT** *waves goodnight to* **MATTIE** *and she let's out a short scream.)*

COUNT. What is it?

(The **COUNT** *looks down at his hand and sees it has turned into a wolf's paw. He also lets out a short scream.)*

MATTIE. What's going on?

COUNT. Apparently I *am* turning into a wolf, but until my internal clocks catch up to it, the transformation will occur annoyingly slow.

MATTIE. That's awful.

COUNT. My right hand is now totally useless. How inconvenient.

MATTIE. You don't have to explain to me.

COUNT. Why don't you go for a long run for a couple of hours.

MATTIE. I wish you wouldn't blow your top all the time.

COUNT. I am not blowing my top! I am a vampire, not a volcano. I hate this place. Of all the places you could suggest we move to…

*(The **COUNT** goes to the window.)*

COUNT *(Continued)* At least there are the bats. There are many bats out tonight, covering the valley like a black shroud. How beautiful they look. Predators on silent wings, bringing death to the unwary…the incautious… the foolish.

MATTIE. They look like they're just eating insects.

(There is a loud explosion accompanied by a bright flash of light.)

MATTIE. Oh my gosh! That bat just blew up!

COUNT. What?! Bats do not just blow up. Not without help. And we are next to an army base, are we not?

*(The **COUNT** exits into another room.)*

MATTIE. What are you going to do?

COUNT *(O.S)* Call the base. Tell them I am coming over.

MATTIE. No, no! You mustn't. What if they expose you.

COUNT *(O.S.)* Very well, I shall put on clean underwear.

MATTIE. I mean, what if they should discover your true identity?

COUNT *(O.S.)* They will be too busy trembling before me to do anything about it.

*(The **COUNT** enters with dozens of little pieces of toilet paper stuck to his face.)*

MATTIE. What happened?!

COUNT. You try shaving your face without being able to see your reflection in the mirror! Tomorrow I am going to grow a beard. Now out of my way.

MATTIE. But what can you do?

COUNT. I shall strangle them with my bare hands.

MATTIE. How? Your right hand is a paw.

COUNT. Then maybe I shall dig up their garden. I do not know. But I will not stand idly by while my relatives are being blown up.

MATTIE. Be careful. Remember, I'll be waiting right here for you. The floor shall be stained with my tears until you return. What do you think of that?

COUNT. I think it is beautiful. I also think it is the only water these floors will ever see. Now goodbye.

MATTIE. Wait.

*(**MATTIE** takes a flower and puts it in the **COUNT**'s lapel. As she forces the flower in the lapel, it tears)*

MATTIE. I know. While you're gone I could buy you something new to wear. What would you like?

COUNT. Camouflage. Now, for the last time, will you go for a long, tiring run. I have important business to attend to.

*(The **COUNT** exits. **MATTIE** takes a small book out of her suitcase and begins writing out loud.)*

MATTIE. Dear Diary, I think the Count is falling in love with me.

(She looks at the flower she is still holding.)

Sort of. I only know I feel closer to him than ever before. I would ask the Count to have Mother and Father over for dinner and a game of cards one night, except, I'm afraid he would only have them for dinner. What to do? What to do?

(BLACKOUT)

End of Scene 1

Scene 2

SETTING: *The living quarters of the Base Commander's home.*

AT RISE: *One hour later.* **COLONEL JOHN PUDDLEPONT** *is standing on top of one of the dining room chairs, holding a small model airplane over the dinner table, dropping grapes. As the grapes drop, he makes a soft whistling sound followed by the sound of muffled explosion.*

MRS. PUDDLEPONT. *(O.S.)* John. Will you help me in the kitchen.

COLONEL. Busy, Dear.

MRS. PUDDLEPONT. *(O.S)* You're not bombing the gravy boat again, are you?

(The **COLONEL** *quickly gets off the chair.)*

COLONEL. No, Dear.

MRS. PUDDLEPONT. *(O.S.)* Because I really don't know what to say to our guests when they find grapes in the gravy.

COLONEL. Yes, Dear.

(The **COLONEL** *"flies" the model back toward the mantle of the fireplace, going out of his way just long enough to "strafe" a large picture of* **MRS. LENORA PUDDLEPONTT** *resting on a table. The doorbell rings.)*

COLONEL *(Continued)* I'll get it.

(The Colonel opens the door and **JOYCE***, neatly dressed, breezes in and is very cheerful.)*

JOYCE. G.A.O.

COLONEL. The General Accounting Office? But it's nine at night.

JOYCE. I know, and all good little taxpayers are fast asleep, aren't they. And it's my job to see that they can continue to sleep knowing that the expenditure of government funds is being carefully scrutinized.

(She walks over by the kitchen.)

JOYCE *(Continued)* Is that steak I smell? Isn't it wonderful that some government employees can have the time and energy to enjoy cookouts at government expense, after a hard day's work. Wonderful. Wonderful.

(She takes out a pad.)

I still have to write that down, but I, for one, think it's just wonderful that our men in uniform can relax after a hard days battle. Wait. I'll have to erase that last part because we're not in a war are we. Silly me.

COLONEL. This is highly irregular!

JOYCE. Beautiful linen tablecloth. Cotton is so dreary. Are there three "a"s in "extravagant"?

COLONEL. That tablecloth was paid for out of my own pocket!

JOYCE. Oh, that *is* a good salary you have. And I believe we can't pay our men in uniform enough during time of war. Wait. There, I go again. There is no war going on, is there.

*(**JOYCE** continues writing in her pad.)*

COLONEL. Now see here…I'm expecting a guest any minute.

*(**JOYCE** continues writing in her pad.)*

JOYCE. And I'm sure she's beautiful.

COLONEL. I'm a married man!

JOYCE. Oh, good. Then the government can look forward to saving at least some money on the dancing girls?

COLONEL. I am not charging the government anything for anyone! I'll dance with my wife!

JOYCE. And what time will the military band be arriving. I do so like "Semper Fidelis." It has a nice beat. Bom… bom…

COLONEL. I haven't called over any military band! Now listen. Carefully. This guest owns property adjacent to the base. He called me! And it's very important to keep on good terms with him. I'm sure I can explain any questions you have later.

JOYCE. Who is this guest exactly?

COLONEL. A Count, of some sort. I don't know any more than that.

JOYCE. Well, very well. I'll leave. I'm almost out of ink anyway. But I'll be questioning you about him tomorrow.

COLONEL. Thank you very much.

JOYCE. Will the electricity be on much longer?

COLONEL. I promise to turn it off as soon as he leaves.

*(The **COLONEL** leads **JOYCE** by the arm towards the front door.)*

JOYCE. You know of course the government pays for electricity. It doesn't come to us in a box on Valentine's Day from the power company.

COLONEL. I know, I know.

*(She exits. The **COLONEL** sits down and fans himself. He sees a lamp on by the desk and quickly jumps up and turns it off. The doorbell rings and he lets the **COUNT** in. The **COUNT** looks very upset)*

COLONEL *(Continued)* Ah! Count Zescu, I believe.

*(The **COLONEL** extends his hand in a greeting but sees the **COUNT** is keeping his right hand in his pocket)*

COUNT. I am sorry, but...

COLONEL. Oh. Battle wound?

COUNT. Let us just say the last time I saw my hand was in a place that needed to be mopped up. Now then...

COLONEL. Well it's an honor to meet you sir.

COUNT. Thank you very much.

COLONEL. Tragic, the things we leave forever buried on the field of honor.

COUNT. True. But I find now it is easier than ever to dig them back up. Now then...

COLONEL. A magnificent attitude, sir. Magnificent!

COUNT. Thank you very much.

COLONEL. Please, take a seat.

COUNT. Oh no. We have plenty at home.

COLONEL. I mean, sit down.

COUNT. Thank you very much.

*(The **COUNT** sits down, uncertain and confused by the **COLONEL**'s apparently friendly attitude.)*

COLONEL. I've taken the liberty of having something prepared for you to eat.

COUNT. Prepared? I must warn you, you would find my tastes somewhat difficult to accommodate.

COLONEL. Oh, I don't know. My wife can make food in 120 different languages.

COUNT. She must own an extraordinary number of cookbooks.

*(**MRS. PUDDLEPONT** enters, from the kitchen.)*

COUNT *(Continued)* But I see she has the rack for it. My apologies.

MRS. PUDDLEPONT. Aren't you going to introduce me to our guest, John?

COLONEL. Of course. This, my dear is…

MRS. PUDDLEPONT. Don't tell me. Count Zescu.

*(The **COUNT** clicks his heels.)*

MRS. PUDDLEPONT. *(Continued)* You have blue blood written all over you.

*(The **COUNT** wipes his mouth with his hand and examines it for any traces of blood.)*

COUNT. I could have sworn I washed.

COLONEL. The Count owns the property adjacent to the base. Must have cost you a pretty penny.

COUNT. My attorney arranged it.

COLONEL. Then it must have really cost you.

COUNT. It began too. But you can rest assured for once it was the client who sucked his attorney dry.

COLONEL. Good for you!

COUNT. Thank you very much.

(They all laugh.)

MRS. PUDDLEPONT. Let me get the food.

COUNT. No, permit me. You have been so kind already.

*(The **COUNT** exits.)*

MRS. PUDDLEPONT. I believe he's the most gracious guest we've ever had over.

COLONEL. Military man. And a great one, at that. Lost his hand in battle.

MRS. PUDDLEPONT. But if he has only one hand, shouldn't we be helping him bring out the food?

*(The sound of several dishes breaking can be heard. **MRS. PUDDLEPONT** starts toward the kitchen, but is held back by the **COLONEL**.)*

COLONEL. No, no my dear. You mustn't. It would shatter him.

(The sound of several more dishes breaking can be heard.)

MRS. PUDDLEPONT. Well, I think he should be used to the sound by now. I've got to go in there.

COLONEL. I forbid it. I know that type of man. Self-reliance is now the most important thing to him. So what's a few dishes…

(The sound of pots and pans falling can be heard.)

COLONEL *(Continued)* …Or pots and pans…

(A loud explosion is heard.)

COLONEL *(Continued)* …Or oven exploding, if it means a measure of self-respect.

*(The **COUNT** enters with a cloud of smoke, carefully balancing several broken dishes on his arm)*

COUNT. Soup's on!

MRS. PUDDLEPONT. *(Looking)* Where?

COUNT. The ceiling. I will clean it up later.

COLONEL. No, no. You are *our* guest. Now please quit troubling yourself over us and tell me why you wanted to see me tonight. It sounded very urgent.

COUNT. Well, looking out my window tonight, I saw a very unusual thing. I saw a bat explode.

COLONEL. Oh. I see. You know something about bats, Count?

COUNT. Well, I haven't been living in a cave *all* my life.

COLONEL. Filthy creatures, bats.

COUNT. What's that?!

*(The **COUNT** quickly brushes off any crumbs that may have fallen on his shirt, and rubs his teeth with his forefinger, trying to brighten them.)*

COLONEL. They smell…

*(The **COUNT** quickly smells under his arm.)*

COLONEL. …Carry diseases…

*(The **COUNT** checks both sides of his hand.)*

COLONEL. …And pollute the wells with their incessant droppings.

COUNT. But there were no service stations to be found on my way over here.

COLONEL. What's that?

COUNT. I say…These army rations are bound to be the best anywhere.

COLONEL. Oh, these aren't ordinary rations. You are a guest. Are you all right, Count? You don't look well.

COUNT. Is nothing, it's just that I don't think you consider all the good, bats do. Take those flowers over there.

*(The **COUNT** walks over to a vase of flowers sitting on a table and picks them up.)*

COLONEL. A hobby of my wife's. What about them?

COUNT. Did you know that many types of bats are responsible for pollinating thousands of different species of flowers and plants. So now what do you say?

COLONEL. I say I'd sacrifice a field of daffodils if I had the opportunity to shoot one bat…

*(The **COUNT** unconsciously starts crushing the flowers.)*

… Peel its wings off…

*(The **COUNT** continues to crush the flowers.)*

… and burn it to a cinder.

*(The **COUNT** shreds the flowers. The **COLONEL** looks at the vase full of shredded and crushed flowers, and the **COUNT** finally sees what he is doing.)*

MRS. PUDDLEPONT. Good heavens, Count!

COUNT. Oh…I…Think they need more water. Let me get some.

COLONEL. Quite all right, Count. Don't trouble yourself.

COUNT. Very well. But about that bat I saw explode…

COLONEL. I'm afraid you're forcing me to reveal myself.

*(The **COLONEL** closes the drapes.)*

COUNT. Please, don't trouble yourself on my account.

COLONEL *(Continued)* Can I count on you, Count?

COUNT. Of course.

*(The **COUNT** offers his hand, spreading his fingers)*

COUNT *(Continued)* But if you're going to count higher than five, I'm afraid I'm going to have to take off my shoes.

COLONEL. No, no. I mean, trust you to keep a secret.

COUNT. What if I promise to take it to the grave with me.

COLONEL. That's good enough for me. Now then, I needn't tell you how important defense is to a country. You know what I mean, Count. Your family had a stake in their country.

COUNT. Actually, my country had a stake in my family.

COLONEL. If you knew the enemy of your country was at your very doorstep, could you sleep at night?

COUNT. No. But then, I usually sleep during the day.

COLONEL. Then you agree. A country prepared, is a country that need never unnecessarily spill the blood of its own citizens.

COUNT. My parents taught me never to waste food.

COLONEL. Well then…We are currently conducting experiments in how to turn bats into flying bombs.

COUNT. That…That is insane!

COLONEL. I know how you feel. Infantry men like ourselves don't need a bunch of smelly bats doing our work for us.

COUNT. Who is in charge of this experiment?

COLONEL. Lt. Crisis. Say I know what will make you feel better. What say tomorrow, me and you get a couple of shotguns and shoot some of the miserable creatures.

COUNT. What?!

COLONEL. Oh, don't worry. We have thousands of the little vermin. Breed faster than rabbits.

COUNT. Apparently they have too! I am leaving now!

COLONEL. I assure you, you are getting excited over nothing. Please, Count, take a seat.

COUNT. Alright. But it will take more than this to make it up to me!

(The **COUNT** *picks up a chair and storms out.)*

MRS. PUDDLEPONT. What an odd fellow.

COLONEL. You have to give him allowances. He's been in battle, you know. He's a real soldier's soldier.

MRS. PUDDLEPONT. I…I must admit he did seem to exude a strange sexual magnetism. Oh, I'm sorry, John.

COLONEL. Don't be. I felt it myself.

(Pause.)

I meant that as a clinical observation, of course.

MRS. PUDDLEPONT. As did I, as did I.

(The **COLONEL** *walks over to a window and looks out wistfully.)*

COLONEL. You're a beautiful woman, Mrs. Puddlepont. I wouldn't blame you for wondering what it might have been like to be married to a Count. Me... I'm just a Colonel.

(She hugs the **COLONEL.***)*

MRS. PUDDLEPONT. You're wrong, John. I'd rather be in the service with you, than serviced by the Count any day.

(Pause, then carefully pronouncing each word)

I mean, in the service, with the Count.

(The **COLONEL** *hugs* **MRS. PUDDLEPONT***, not seeing that* **MRS. PUDDLEPONT** *is biting her lip.)*

COLONEL. The army means nothing to me, my dear. I'd rather be with you, than handle the privates of an entire command.

(Pause, then carefully pronouncing each word.)

I mean, in charge of all the privates I could command.

*(***MRS. PUDDLEPONT** *hugs the* **COLONEL***, not seeing that the* **COLONEL** *is biting his lip.)*

(A howl of a wolf is heard in the distance.)

(BLACKOUT)

End of Scene 2

Scene 3

SETTING: *A laboratory, with several cages holding bats quietly resting and hanging upside down.*

AT RISE: *One hour later.* **LT. CRISIS** *is hunched over one cage trying to feed a bat, softly cajoling it as one might a baby.* **DR. GUNTER,** *who speaks with a thick German accent, is impatiently standing next to him.*

LT. CRISIS. Come on. Come on. You can eat it. Nice yummy food. Oh yes, nice yummy food.

DR. GUNTER. Lieutenant, please. I am starting to feel sick.

LT. CRISIS. Oh, I'm sorry. Shall I open a window.

DR. GUNTER. Only if you promise to fling yourself through it! I mean enough mit ze baby talk!

LT. CRISIS. I think it's important to establish a rapport with them. Remember, these bats have been removed from their natural habitat, and some require a little extra attention and understanding.

DR. GUNTER. Lieutenant. Ze fact zat you believe zat, does you credit. Ze fact zat I am calmly listening to you instead of striking you, does me credit. Undt ze fact zat ze bat does not confuse you for its mother does it credit. Do you see vhat I'm getting at?

LT. CRISIS. *(Thinking)* That as long as we all do what we believe is right…we can never go wrong?

DR. GUNTER. Nein, mine son. Vhat I am trying to say is… That I will eat ze food mineself if you do not make mit ze progress report!

LT. CRISIS. But…

DR. GUNTER. Give me ze food!

*(**DR. GUNTER** grabs the plate and swallows the food.)*

There! It is done! Now then Lieutenant we can get back to work.

(Pause)

But first you vill tell me vhat I have just eaten.

LT. CRISIS. The thorax of a grasshopper.

(Pause)

Would you like a glass of water?

DR. GUNTER. Now there's an idea.

*(**LT. CRISIS** brings **DR. GUNTER** a glass of water.)*

LT. CRISIS. And frankly sir, I don't mean to be curt with you, but I've only requisitioned enough grasshoppers for the bats.

DR. GUNTER. I vasn't planning to ask for seconds.

LT. CRISIS. *(Muttering)* Grasshoppers are hard to find right now. They're only sexually active one month of the year, you know.

DR. GUNTER. I don't doubt it. If mine wife tasted like zat, it vould take me 11 months to vork up ze courage to kiss her also.

*(**DR. GUNTER** spits.)*

But I am not here to discuss the frequency of sexual encounters between physically repulsive creatures.

LT. CRISIS. Oh no sir, you're being too hard on your…

DR. GUNTER. I am talking about ze grasshoppers!

LT. CRISIS. Oh…well…uh…I think you'll be pleased with the results of today's experiments.

*(**JOYCE** walks in wearing overalls, carrying a fumigation canister.)*

JOYCE. Pest control.

DR. GUNTER. Vhat is ze meaning of zis? No one is allowed in here! Did you not read ze sign?

JOYCE. No, and don't tell me the plot. I was going to take it home with me and read it before bed. Now let's get out of here.

*(**DR. GUNTER** takes her to the sign.)*

DR. GUNTER. I vill interpret. No entrance!

JOYCE. Look, *I* understand what it says, but *termites* can't read.

LT. CRISIS. Termites?

JOYCE. Yep. This foundation is under more pressure than Aunt Lilly's support hose. But don't worry. This little baby is going to release more gas than Uncle Harry at a chili convention. Say, they're both down in the car. Maybe you'd like to meet them while your friend checks with the Colonel?

LT. CRISIS. No, no that's ok. But to fumigate here? Our bats would die.

JOYCE. Well then, I'm just going to have to charge you extra. I only came for the termites.

LT. CRISIS. I'm sorry, but until we have time to relocate our test subjects, fumigation is out of the question.

JOYCE. Ok, I'll leave but I'll still have to charge you. I'm on the clock. And Colonel Puddlepont hates waste. Hates it.

LT. CRISIS. Oh. But can't you treat them locally? From downstairs?

JOYCE. Well…seeing how tomorrow is Valentine's Day, and I feel good…Ok! I'll kill the little bastards with spray. Pine scented, you know. Makes you glad to be alive. What are you guys doing anyway?

LT. CRISIS. Well…

DR. GUNTER. Ve are trying to get on mit our business. Now goodbye.

(She exits.)

DR. GUNTER. Now then Lieutenant, tell me *please*. Has ze reduced weight of ze high-explosive ze bats are carrying proved useful?

LT. CRISIS. Oh, yes. Hardly any of them have to be driven to the target area in the major's car anymore.

DR. GUNTER. Zis is goot. The major vas beginning to complain about ze odor inside his car.

LT. CRISIS. Gee, I thought he'd be more upset than that.

DR. GUNTER. Not at all. I assured him your personal struggle with body odor vas a valiant one undt vould soon prove successful.

LT. CRISIS. My personal struggle… !

DR. GUNTER. Lieutenant, please. We need not give ze major a reason to cancel zis project. He is already quite unhappy about it. And if we inform him of every little setback he vill never let us finish. The point is, ze bats are now able to fly with ze explosive strapped beneath them.

LT. CRISIS. The point is, the major now thinks my personal hygiene requires attention.

DR. GUNTER. You are being too sensitive. I am sure he has forgotten all about it.

LT. CRISIS. I hope so.

DR. GUNTER. By the way, here is some extra strength soap the major wanted me to give you.

LT. CRISIS. What?!

DR. GUNTER. Lieutenant, you vill please stop thinking of your own personal problems, undt give me today's progress report.

LT. CRISIS. Well, experiments with Flappy have proven…

DR. GUNTER. Flappy? Ach der Lieber! How many times have I told you not to name ze experimental subjects. You must be a detached scientist. Zese are not your friends like you undt me Bill.

LT. CRISIS. Herbert.

DR. GUNTER. Ze point is to be detached. For instance, Vhat if ze government of ze United States vas suddenly overthrown undt I was ordered to perform strange experiments on ze defeated, helpless soldiers of ze American army. Such as…oh…I don't know…

(DR. GUNTER begins feeling the joints of the LIEUTENANT's torso, and moving his appendages.)

…Surgically removing their legs undt replacing them with ze transplanted appendages of a gazelle, creating a rapid deployment infantry soldier. Hmmmm…how is ze government of ze great United States doing these days?

LT. CRISIS. Just fine.

DR. GUNTER. *(Disappointed)* Oh.

LT. CRISIS. But I think I see your point.

DR. GUNTER. Yah, ze legs of a gazelle would…

LT. CRISIS. I mean your other point. I…I can't let myself get personally attached to the test subjects. After all, it's not like you and me.

DR. GUNTER. Zat is right, Bobby.

LT. CRISIS. Herbert.

DR. GUNTER. Yah, yah, yah.

LT. CRISIS. It's just the lack of resources…

DR. GUNTER. *(Interrupts)* Resources! Zat is no excuse!

LT. CRISIS. Anyway, the weight of the explosives has dropped to the point where these bats can now travel considerable distances.

DR. GUNTER. Undt how vill they be directed to ze target?

LT. CRISIS. This bat has learned to associate large insect populations with the shape and color of an enemy's helmet. It has been conditioned to seek out the enemy by following its most basic instinct – Hunger.

DR. GUNTER. Excellent! But where did you get ze enemy helmet?

LT. CRISIS. Well, we didn't have any on hand. So uh, to facilitate the experiment…

*(**LT. CRISIS** pulls out a German army helmet from a box.)*

DR. GUNTER. Mine old army helmet? You ver in mine room without mine authorization?

LT. CRISIS. Well…

DR. GUNTER. I am a naturalized citizen now! Ze Var is over! How much longer must I be subjected to zese indignities!

LT. CRISIS. I meant no disrespect. I just wanted to speed up the research, and when I found your box of old war souvenirs you've kept...like your helmet...

DR. GUNTER. I vas going to make it into a flowerpot.

(**LT. CRISIS** *pulls out a gun from the box.*)

LT. CRISIS. ...Your lugar converted to silently fire poison pellets...

DR. GUNTER. A gift from mine father for mine confirmation.

(**LT. CRISIS** *pulls out a letter from the box.*)

LT. CRISIS. ...And a letter of commendation from the German High Command on your plan to assassinate President Roosevelt...

DR. GUNTER. You do not get letters of commendation from ze German High Command for inventing a new recipe for strudel! Unless of course, it vas for der Furher's birthday. I vas young. Undt ambitious. But those times are past. I have nothing to hide.

(**DR. GUNTER** *strikes the desk with his fist with his hand and several daggers fall out of his sleeves.*)

DR. GUNTER. Oh...I vas vondering where I put those. No vonder I can never find a letter opener vhen I need von.

(**LT. CRISIS** *is preoccupied with a bat in a cage.*)

LT. CRISIS. Of course. And I think you'll find the experiment most instructive. Now if you'll just put on this helmet and stand on the other side of the room. I'll open the window and release the bat. You will find, that even when presented with the opportunity to fly to freedom the bat will go towards you instead.

(**LT. CRISIS** *opens a window and prepares to open the bat's cage.* **DR. GUNTER** *stands on the opposite side of the room, next to a large globe of the world. With the helmet on his head,* **DR. GUNTER** *starts remembering fonder times. He strokes the surface of the globe slowly, almost passionately, and starts softly humming the Third Reich national anthem. he stops and looks closely* *at the globe.)*

LT. CRISIS. Ready, Dr. Gunter?

DR. GUNTER. *(Bitterly)* Yes. I am ready. I vas ready at ze Rhine, vhen Capt. Steiner retreated, and left me behind to be captured by ze filthy American swine…

*(**DR. GUNTER** stops. Sees **LT. CRISIS** look at him quizzically. **DR. GUNTER** regains his composure.)*

DR. GUNTER. Ready, vhen you are, mine gracious American host.

LT. CRISIS. Prepare to witness history!

*(**LT. CRISIS** opens the door of the cage, and the bat immediately flies out of the window.)*

DR. GUNTER. Humph! Lieutenant Crisis, I must inform you zat your bat is not on ze ball.

*(**LT. CRISIS** walks over to the window.)*

LT. CRISIS. I don't understand it. Maybe he's just resting.

*(**DR. GUNTER** joins **LT. CRISIS** by the window.)*

DR. GUNTER. I'm afraid it is more serious than zat. You have struck out mit your bat and now, for both of us I'm afraid, it is back to the ze minors.

*(The **COUNT** pops up from behind the window.)*

COUNT. Did somebody say minors?

(Pause)

Oh fudge!

LT. CRISIS. A spy!

COUNT. A spy am I? What would you say if I could turn into a wolf, leap through this window and tear out your throat with a single bite of my massive, powerful, slathering jaws?

(He looks at his watch)

Eventually.

LT. CRISIS. I'd say I'd have to shoot you.

*(**LT. CRISIS** pulls out a gun)*

COUNT. And what if I said your bullets would have no effect on me.

(**LT. CRISIS** *puts the gun to the* **COUNT***'s head.*)

LT. CRISIS. I'd say I'd have to give back the silver bullets I won for winning a shooting competition.

COUNT. Silver bullets? Hmmm. Not really my Achilles heel. But you never really know and - seeing as I am wearing my best suit - very well. You have just captured yourself a spy. Now help me through this window.

(**LT. CRISIS** *and* **DR. GUNTER** *help the* **COUNT** *through the window.*)

COUNT *(Continued)* Thank you very much…Lt. Crisis.

LT. CRISIS. You know me?

COUNT. I know of you. And if you're going to keep that gun pointed at me, you might inform Colonel Puddlepont.

(**LT. CRISIS** *goes to a phone leaving* **DR. GUNTER** *and the* **COUNT** *staring at each other*)

DR. GUNTER. I don't believe it! It has been a long time, Count Zescu.

COUNT. Yes…I thought I smelled a rat…Dr… .

DR. GUNTER. Gunter. Here, mine name is Dr. Gunter.

COUNT. I wonder what the Americans would think if they knew your real name. I doubt they would provide you with such comfortable accommodations.

DR. GUNTER. And I vonder vhat ze Colonel vould say if he knew *your* real identity. He is not exactly crazy about bats, as it is.

(**LT. CRISIS** *hangs up the phone and addresses the* **COUNT** *and* **DR. GUNTER.**)

LT. CRISIS. I'm sorry. He is a friend of the Colonel's. I'll be right back. The Colonel wants to see him.

(**LT. CRISIS** *exits.*)

DR. GUNTER. Zis is no way to treat an old friend. You vill forgive me, Count.

COUNT. Certainly. You can hardly be blamed for possessing the appearance of a baboon.

(**DR. GUNTER** *reaches for his old German lugar.*)

DR. GUNTER. A baboon mit a gun, if you vill. It is time to end vhat vas begun fifteen years ago. Auf wiedersehen, Count.

(**DR. GUNTER** *fires the gun at the* **COUNT**. *The* **COUNT** *calmly removes a poison dart from his shoulder.*)

COUNT. Sorry. But this poison dart has even less effect on me than your wife's cooking.

DR. GUNTER. You vill leave mine wife out of this!

COUNT. It hurts, doesn't it?

DR. GUNTER. No, no, no! Stop! I do not wish to hear anymore! But at least I have had a wife. Something you can never know anything about. Something, soft and radiant…comforting…keeping you warm on cold nights…

COUNT. Believe me, keeping warm on cold nights has not been a problem lately. Would you believe I got a sunburn last night?

DR. GUNTER. Vhat?

COUNT. It is a long story. And I'm afraid you no longer have the time to hear it. As you say, we must now end what was begun fifteen years ago. I shall now turn into a wolf, leap on you and rip out your throat with one bite of my jaws.

(*He looks at his watch.*)

Oh phooey!

(*The* **COUNT** *punches* **DR. GUNTER** *in the face, and he goes flying backwards and falls down unconscious. The* **COUNT** *is surprised by the result and looks at his fist.*)

COUNT (*Continued*) Say, that was pretty good!

(*The bats in the cages begin to emit high pitch squeaking. The* **COUNT** *turns towards them.*)

COUNT *(Continued)* Do not worry, my children. I shall set you free.

*(The **COUNT** goes to the cages to open them but finds they are locked.)*

COUNT *(Continued)* Drat! The Lieutenant must have the key. Come on boys.

*(The **COUNT** stacks the cages, one on top of the other and struggles towards the door with them, stepping over **DR. GUNTER**'s still unconscious body. A bat in one of the cages emits some high pitched squeaking.)*

COUNT *(Continued)* What do you mean he ate your supper? No, we are not going to stop somewhere first to get a bite to eat. Yes, of course I know grasshoppers are hard to find this time of year. What's that? No! I will not rescue you tomorrow night after you've had dinner! We are leaving now.

*(As the **COUNT** reaches the door, the **COLONEL** and **LT. CRISIS** step in. The **COLONEL** is holding a document. He and **LT. CRISIS** look at the **COUNT** holding the cages)*

COLONEL. I'm afraid I don't understand this.

*(The **COUNT** takes the document from the **COLONEL**.)*

COUNT. Well, let me read it myself and I will get back to you tomorrow. Goodbye.

COLONEL. I mean, what are you doing with our bats?

COUNT. Oh, well I remember how you talked about us going after the filthy things...

(The bats emit more high-pitched squeaking.)

Yes, yes, even though I know they spend hours every day grooming themselves...and well, I thought I would get some...target practice. I hope there is no problem with that?

LT. CRISIS. You were going to shoot them while they were in a cage?

COUNT. Well...yes...But I was going to give them an hour's head start.

COLONEL. I knew there was good explanation! You're my kind of man, Count. Except these bats are very valuable to us. Which is why I'm glad I found you. By the way, where's is Dr. Gunter?

(DR. GUNTER *moans from behind a piece of furniture.*
LT. CRISIS *and the* COLONEL *run to his side.*)

COLONEL. What happened?

DR. GUNTER. I vas struck...

COUNT. Struck?

DR. GUNTER. (*Looking at the* COUNT.) Struck...mit a case of ze dizzys. I am perfectly all right.

COLONEL. A very strange night, indeed. My wife is in a similar state. Some damn fool dog dug up her garden.

DR. GUNTER. Tell me Count, is zat a petunia in your pocket?

COUNT. I do not believe now is the time for physical comparisons...

(DR. GUNTER *pulls a flower out of the* COUNT*'s pocket.*)

COUNT (*Continued*) Oh wait. It is a petunia. Er...for your wife, Colonel.

COLONEL. Very gracious of you. Petunias are just what my wife lost.

COUNT. Really? What an amazing coincidence!

COLONEL. Yes, but I don't think it was a dog that dug them up. By the sound of the howl I heard, I think it was more like a wolf. Which actually suits me fine.

COUNT. I am glad to hear at least you enjoy...

COLONEL. Always wanted to kill a wolf.

COUNT. ...A nice hobby.

COLONEL. But I was glad to hear you were still around, Count. This document is a contract. The military would like to lease part of your land. We need more space for our test subjects. Bats aren't the brightest creatures you know.

COUNT. This has been one of those days where I might be inclined to agree with you. But what if we discuss it at my house during dinner tomorrow night. Yes. Say around midnight. When I will be more myself.

COLONEL. An unusual time. But I'm happy to agree to it.

DR. GUNTER. I think lunch time mineself, vould be more appropriate. Say on ze veranda under ze bright noontime sun. Eh, Count?

(**DR. GUNTER** *puts his arm around the* **COUNT**.)

COUNT. Noontime? You mean when the military archives are open and we can peruse old war documents after we are finished eating?

(*The* **COUNT** *puts his arm around* **DR. GUNTER**.)

COLONEL. Say, I like that idea!

DR. GUNTER. Nein, nein. I have just remembered an appointment mit mine foot specialist. Midnight at your house vill be fine, Count.

COLONEL. Oh come now, how long could it possibly take to see a foot Doctor?

COUNT. Well when you do as much running as Dr. Gunter, who can say.

COLONEL. Very well. Midnight at your house Count. I need something to relax me.

COUNT. I assure you, after you come you will find it difficult to leave.

COLONEL. Good. Because after you left I got a call from my brother-in-law.

(*The* **COUNT** *leads them to the door, smiling and anticipating tomorrow night.*)

COLONEL (*Continued*) Frantic he was. Still hasn't heard a word from his daughter, my niece, since she became a foreign exchange student.

COUNT. Foreign exchange student?

COLONEL. Story is she ran away with an older man.

COUNT. Older man?

COLONEL. Right. And if you think I've got it in for bats and wolves, wait till I get my hands on that pervert.

COUNT. Pervert?

COLONEL. Mattie's only seventeen.

*(The **COLONEL** walks from underneath the **COUNT**'s arm and exits with everybody else. The **COUNT**'s arm is still frozen as though still around the **COLONEL**'s shoulder. The **COUNT** is frozen too. The **COLONEL** returns.)*

COLONEL. Coming Count? Good heavens, what's wrong.

COUNT. Is nothing. I think I just remembered I left something running at the house.

COLONEL. Oh. The water?

COUNT. Must be, because I feel like I am up the creek.

*(The **COLONEL** starts turning off the lights in the office.)*

COLONEL. Well, better get home and turn it off.

COUNT. I do not even know how I turned it on. I think it has a screw loose.

COLONEL. Hope you manage. Modern conveniences are very expensive in the desert. Cost you an arm and a leg, if you're not careful.

COUNT. You would have to put it that way.

*(The **COLONEL** leads the **COUNT** to the door, looks around briefly and turns off the last light and only light shining from outside penetrates the room through the window. One beam illuminates a ventilation shaft on the floor. After a moment it is forced open and **JOYCE** crawls through, with a flashlight, and speaks in a small portable tape-recorder and sings)*

JOYCE. This is Joyce Lyonhartt for the Herald Tribune. Dateline – Heatstroke, California. I have located Count Zescu. To all the mothers and fathers of the world – Watch your children. Vampires do exist. Though this one seems about as dangerous as lemon juice on a paper cut. Yet, his very existence has been placed in jeopardy from several quarters.

(She stands up and walks around the room continuing to talk into her recorder.)

JOYCE *(Continued)* I am besieged by conflicting and morally ambiguous questions. This is Joyce Lyonhartt reporting from Heatstroke, California.

(BLACKOUT)

End of Act I

ACT 2

Scene 1

SETTING: *The main living room of the* **COUNT***'s estate.*

AT RISE: *The next evening, just before midnight.* **MATTIE***, wearing a very sexy robe, is pacing back and forth reading from a book while spraying herself with perfume.*

MATTIE. "The common male vampire bat, or Desmodus Rotundus, initiates its courtship ritual by firmly grasping the female on the back of her neck with his mouth"... Oh my!

(She sprays some perfume on the back of her neck, and continues to read)

MATTIE *(Continued)* "The actual sex act usually lasts anywhere from one to three minutes though it has never been observed to last longer than four." Men! But maybe if the poor thing wasn't being observed all the time...it might not be so shy! Only if I could talk to my mother.

(She goes over to the open window and closes it. A second later a bat slams into the window from outside, and bounces off and falls down with an audible THUMP. **MATTIE** *quickly opens the window as the* **COUNT** *staggers up into view holding his hand on his head)*

MATTIE *(Continued)* Oh darling, I'm sorry. I should always keep the window open, so my sweet beloved can fly to me on speedy wings whenever his heart grows lonely.

COUNT. And just what window did you bump your head against?

(**MATTIE** *helps the* **COUNT** *through the window.*)

MATTIE. You should wear your glasses like the Doctor says. He says you're as blind as a bat without them.

(*The* **COUNT** *just stares at her.*)

But what does he know. Anyway, I was so worried about you. Where have you been for the past 24 hours?

COUNT. In the dog pound. Would you believe it? As soon as I turn into a wolf, I get picked up for not having a license.

MATTIE. It must have been terrible.

COUNT. Yes, I had to come all the way home to get a concussion. It was the first good night's sleep I've had since I've arrived here!

MATTIE. (*Opening up her robe*) Want to try for two in a row?

COUNT. Not with you I do not! You have kept a secret from me!

MATTIE. You found out. Ok, I'm sorry. But I *need* to hire help to keep a place this large clean.

COUNT. That is not what I am talking about! I am talking about…you mean somebody actually has been helping you clean this place? I hope you have not paid them.

MATTIE. Six dollars. But what other secret are you talking about?

COUNT. That your true age is not twenty-one but in fact… Six dollars? For this? You did not pay in cash?

MATTIE. Yes, I did. And yes, you're right. I'm not twenty-one. I'm only seventeen. But the heart of a woman knows no age, save what makes it beat passionately and strong, for then it lives eternal.

COUNT. American dollars, or Canadian?

MATTIE. American.

COUNT. You have been taken advantage of.

(**MATTIE** *hugs the* **COUNT**.)

MATTIE. I know. And who could blame you?

(The clock begins striking off the hours.)

COUNT. Uncle Puddlepont, that's who.

MATTIE. You met Uncle?

COUNT. I did. And he will be here any second.

(The sound of a car pulling up is heard, as its headlights momentarily shine through the window.)

COUNT *(Continued)* You must stay in the basement until he leaves!

MATTIE. What are you going to do?

*(The **COUNT** drags **MATTIE** to the basement door, and opens it.)*

COUNT. I suppose you would object if I were to hang him and his entire party on meat hooks while I tortured them during dinner?

MATTIE. Of course I would!

*(The **COUNT** takes several meat hooks out of his coat and throws them down.)*

COUNT. Ok, *you* think of something!

(There is a knock on the door.)

MATTIE. Act gracious, serve them dinner, and send them home.

COUNT. You know...that is just crazy enough to work.

*(The **COUNT** shoves **MATTIE** through the basement door, and closes it. He then quickly runs to the front door and opens it as **JOYCE** walks through.)*

COUNT. Who are you?

JOYCE. I'm Joyce Lyonhartt. I was here last night and I've decided it was only fair to warn you...

COUNT. So *you* are the one! This house is still a mess. You are a disgrace to your profession, a blot on vocational training and a menace to everything but dust and dirt, which you apparently view with, unbridled reverence! The only things that have been polished in this room are the seats of the chairs, which, now that I see you, makes me believe you can at least do that efficiently. And now, you have the arrogance to warn me, Count Zescu?! Of what?!

JOYCE. You have a piece of corn stuck between your teeth.

COUNT. Oh.

(The **COUNT** *quickly picks at his teeth with his fingernail.)*

COUNT. Is that better?

JOYCE. Well those long sharp ones are impressive. Remind me to call you if I lose my can opener.

COUNT. The sight of you bringing your can over here is a treat I can live without.

JOYCE. Hey pal, the expiration date may have passed, but you'd be surprised at the amount of guys who still want to read the label.

COUNT. And I am sure not one of them would need to use a magnifying glass either.

JOYCE. You know…if I owned a set of teeth that could attract a lovesick beaver from 100 miles off on a dark night, I wouldn't open my mouth more than I had to.

COUNT. Do not tempt me to accommodate you. But for now I must insist you begin making up for last night. I have company coming. Prepare four place settings. And polish the tops of all the tables. They are filthy.

JOYCE. *(Thoughtfully)* Only four place settings…

COUNT. Well, I would invite you also but I assumed you would be too busy raiding my liquor cabinet to attend. Or am I incorrect in this?

JOYCE. Hmm? No. That's the time when I raid the liquor cabinet all right. But if I can get an early start charging personal long distance phone calls to your number, maybe I can join you for dessert.

COUNT. You may *be* the dessert! You will let in the guests when they arrive. I will go upstairs.

(The **COUNT** *walks towards the staircase.)*

COUNT *(Continued)* I need time to make myself presentable.

JOYCE. Hey, is this dinner for tonight or next year?

*(The **COUNT** stops, holds his temper and proceeds upstairs. As soon as he is out of sight, **JOYCE** takes out her tape recorder and begins talking into it.)*

JOYCE. This is Joyce Lyonhartt reporting from inside Count Zescu's estate. I have decided against warning the Count about the danger, which surrounds him. Is it because as a reporter I believe that interfering with the natural course of events makes me responsible for consequences I can neither predict nor judge? Or is it because the Count implied I possessed a large butt?

*(**JOYCE** tries to look at her reflection in the window.)*

Either way, this bat is a turkey. And I need a drink.

*(**JOYCE** puts away here tape recorder and exits into the kitchen. There is a knock on the door. It becomes persistent and the **COUNT** returns downstairs, buttoning his collar and muttering to himself.)*

COUNT. *(Loudly in no particular direction)* Do not worry. I see you are busy not working. I will get it!

*(The **COUNT** opens the door and greets the **COLONEL**, who is standing on the other side, holding a bottle of wine in one hand and a plate of eclairs in the other. The **COLONEL** is preoccupied with shinning his shoes against his pant-leg. Without looking up, he hands the **COUNT** a bottle of wine, which the **COUNT** takes with his left hand. The **COLONEL** then hands the **COUNT** a plate of eclairs, which the **COUNT** takes with his right hand.)*

COUNT *(Continued)* You shouldn't have...

COLONEL. *(Without looking up)* Nonsense...Just thought I'd give you a hand with the meal.

COUNT. Yes, well...I could always use an extra hand... Whoops!

*(The **COUNT** suddenly realizes he is holding a plate of*

eclairs with his right hand, and immediately stuffs the plate into his right coat pocket, along with the eclairs and his hand. The **COLONEL** *looks up.)*

COLONEL. Damn dirt roads. Hard to keep a good shine. Say, didn't I just hand you some eclairs?

COUNT. *(Pause)* Yes.

COLONEL. Where are they?

COUNT. Oh…Did you want one too?

COLONEL. You mean you ate them already?

COUNT. I have low blood sugar.

COLONEL. I'm sorry, I didn't know. I thought, however, I brought them over on a pla…

(The **COUNT** *quickly pulls the Colonel into the house and shuts the door. The* **COUNT** *puts down the wine.)*

COUNT. You are alone?

COLONEL. Yes, well the Lieutenant isn't really needed for this, and my wife had a headache and I haven't seen Dr. Gunter all day. But I have his old army helmet and a few other things in my car to help explain what we intend to do. Have you seen my new Ford Crown Victoria? Love that car.

COUNT. Then I guess you would like to get back on the road so…

COLONEL. But we haven't even begun.

(The **COLONEL** *sits down.)*

Heard from my brother-in-law again. You know, I can't help thinking at least when I'm through I have a home to go to. Oh, Mattie… !

COUNT. *(Turning around)* Where?

COLONEL. Who knows? I hate to think where my niece could be right now. Maybe I wasn't a good uncle. She was such a spirited girl, going this way and that. Hard to stay on top of her.

COUNT. I believe you are on top of her now.

COLONEL. What do you mean?

LT. Colonel!

(There is general commotion.)

COLONEL. Just a minute! Dr. Gunter. Dr. Gunter, can you hear me? Oh no! Dr. Gunter is playing chess but can't hear any of us, which means that somehow...we must all be dead! Good Heavens, I hope I wasn't buried in this!

*(**LT. CRISIS** feels **DR. GUNTER**'s pulse.)*

LT. Nobody's dead. The Doctor is just unconscious.

COLONEL. You have some explaining to do, Count! What's going on here? Without diagrams, drawings, or sock puppets explain to me straight out, what is going on!

COUNT. *(Getting up)* Very well. I will explain.

(BLACKOUT)

End of Act II Scene I

COUNT. I mean I am sure she is doing well. And I feel that the two of you are closer to each other than you can possibly imagine. So you must not worry…

COLONEL. How can I not? I mean just talking about her… I swear I can actually smell the particular fragrance she always wore.

COUNT. *(Smelling the air)* Yes, a kind of a…

(Quickly)

Well goodnight, it was nice seeing you. We must do this again sometime.

COLONEL. But what about dinner?

COUNT. No thank you, I have already eaten.

COLONEL. But what about the lease?

COUNT. I must apologize for letting you travel this distance for nothing. I have no intention of leasing my land to you for your continued experiments with bats. I am sorry but…

COLONEL. Oh, blast the bats!

COUNT. Blast the bats?

COLONEL. Why don't we sit down on the couch for the moment?

COUNT. But…

COLONEL. We can talk here or some other room. I've never seen your house. Perhaps a tour…

COUNT. No, no, the couch will be the most comfortable place to talk. Now what is it?

*(The **COLONEL** sits on the couch and the **COUNT** joins him.)*

You know, I'm afraid I wasn't altogether honest with you when I told you my wife couldn't make it tonight because she had a headache. You see, I never told my wife I was going to be coming here in the first place.

COUNT. I do not understand.

COLONEL. She still doesn't understand how a couple of military men like us might wish to relive old times.

In the heat of a battle a bond between men becomes forged inside a foxhole.

(The **COLONEL** *moves closer to the* **COUNT***. The* **COUNT** *thinks a second, and then moves farther from the* **COLONEL***.)*

COUNT. Well, I have been inside a few holes in my time. But I usually made sure they were empty first.

COLONEL. I'm talking about the bond that grows between battle hardened veterans for whom the risk of death hangs over them like a heavy shroud…or bedspread, if you like.

(The **COLONEL** *moves closer to the* **COUNT***. The* **COUNT** *thinks a second, and again moves farther from the* **COLONEL***.)*

COUNT. Bedspread?

COLONEL. Say a black satin one.

(The **COLONEL** *moves a closer to the* **COUNT***. The* **COUNT** *immediately moves farther from the* **COLONEL** *to the edge of the couch.)*

COLONEL *(Continued)* I don't know how to put it. But it would help if you would permit me to address you a little less formally, Count.

COUNT. No! Formal or not, I have dressed myself since I was 18.

COLONEL. What I'm trying to say is that there are things we all wish for. Haven't you ever wished for anything?

COUNT. You mean besides a longer couch?

(The **COLONEL** *spills a drink on his uniform.)*

COLONEL. Dear me. I must change out of this immediately. Don't go.

COUNT. I'll be waiting.

(The **COLONEL** *exits up the staircase.)*

Back in Transylvania.

(The **COUNT** *removes his hand from his pocket and*

quickly cleans off the mashed eclairs from them and runs to the front door and opens it, only to find **MRS. PUDDLEPONT**, *who breezes in as he jams his right hand back into his pocket.*)

COUNT *(Continued)* Mrs. Puddlepont!

MRS. PUDDLEPONT. Excuse me for coming over this way, but my husband's not around and I had to warn you about something. I don't know how to begin but John is...

COUNT. I know, I know.

MRS. PUDDLEPONT. ...A huge bore. And you on the other hand are quite exciting to me.

COUNT. Oh fiddlesticks!

MRS. PUDDLEPONT. I've never done anything like this before. My mind's a whirl, but I couldn't let another moment pass without telling you how I feel. My heart is swollen with love for you.

(*The* **COUNT** *looks at her breasts.*)

COUNT. I see. But aside from giving you the name of my tailor there is nothing I can do for you.

(*The* **COUNT** *takes* **MRS. PUDDLEPONT** *by the arm and leads her to the door.*)

MRS. PUDDLEPONT. Then just one last dance. Please, Count. I don't go around planing these things. It just happened.

COUNT. But...but I do not have any music.

(**MRS. PUDDLEPONT** *pulls a record out of her purse, and puts it in a phonograph. A Tango is heard. She takes a rose out of her purse and places it between her teeth. After a few moments of dancing,* **JOYCE** *enters, becomes alarmed and quickly switches records, and starts calling out a square-dance.*)

COUNT. What the...!

MRS. PUDDLEPONT. How charming! A square dance.

JOYCE.
>Ladies curtsey, Gents please bow,
>Then slip away from his somehow,
>Don't let him get too close to you,
>You'll be sorry if you do!
>
>Swing your partner 'round and 'round
>Then run away and don't be found,
>The man you're dancin' with tonight,
>Doesn't kiss but he just might bite

COUNT. What an odd song!

MRS. PUDDLEPONT. But what a lovely melody. Hold me closer.

JOYCE.
>Promenade and dosey do,
>Then try to step on his big toe,
>Under his arms now just slide,
>But don't get stuck you're kinda wide.
>
>One step forward two steps back,
>Be prepared for his attack,
>His teeth are twice as long as yours,
>And could open up a can of Coors.

COUNT. The lyrics sound rather violent for a square-dance.

MRS. PUDDLEPONT. I can only hear the beating of our hearts. Or MY heart, anyway…

JOYCE.
>Swing your partner to the right,
>The spot you're in is very tight,
>Poke his eyes out if you can,
>Then hit him with a fryin' pan.
>
>Listen gal, to what I said,
>You'd better try and use your head,
>Bites on the neck aren't too much fun,
>You'd better just high-tail and run.
>
>Now, I gotta go and find my gun,
>But you'd better just high-tail and run.

(JOYCE *winks at* **MRS. PUDDLEPONT** *and exits.* **MRS. PUDDLEPONT** *looks at the* **COUNT** *quizzically.*)

COUNT. Cleaning lady. Been polishing the tables. Too many fumes I think. Well now you really have to go.

MRS. PUDDLEPONT. Then you're sending me back to my husband?

COUNT. Noooooo, I am sending you back home.

MRS. PUDDLEPONT. You're telling me there is someone else, then?

(Some creaking of the floorboards is heard upstairs.)

COUNT. Well, you have caught me. So you see, you must really leave now…

(Some even louder creaking of the floorboards is heard. **MRS. PUDDLEPONT** *looks up, a little baffled.)*

COUNT *(Continued)* I appreciate a full figured lover.

MRS. PUDDLEPONT. I'll wager everything I own, your paramour is a thing of rare beauty.

COUNT. My advice to you is to get a good night's sleep and to stay away from racetracks.

(The **COUNT** *opens the front door and* **MRS. PUDDLEPONT** *looks outside and quickly shuts it, remaining inside.)*

MRS. PUDDLEPONT. Oh no!

COUNT. What is it?

MRS. PUDDLEPONT. It's Lieutenant Crisis. I could never explain what I am doing here alone this time of night. If he tells my husband…

COUNT. But we haven't done anything.

MRS. PUDDLEPONT. It wouldn't matter to John. The gloves would come off.

COUNT. He did seem to be in a hurry to undress.

MRS. PUDDLEPONT. You've got to hide me.

COUNT. For a moment only. I will get rid of the Lieutenant and then you must leave. You can hide upstairs.

*(The **COUNT** takes her to the foot of the staircase and quickly stops.)*

COUNT *(Continued)* No. Wait. In the cellar.

*(The **COUNT** takes her to the door to the cellar and again quickly stops.)*

COUNT *(Continued)* No. Wait. In the closet.

*(The **COUNT** pushes her in the closet. There is a knock on the front door and the **COUNT** answers it, and **LT. CRISIS** walks through carrying a large bundle of papers.)*

LT. CRISIS. Sorry to disturb you, Sir. But I thought the Colonel would need these latest results. He doesn't like to get behind.

COUNT. Haven't spent much time with the Colonel, have you?

LT. CRISIS. Long enough to know he likes everybody to keep up their end.

COUNT. Well tonight I have a feeling he is going to be disappointed.

LT. CRISIS. Is the…Colonel here?

COUNT. Upstairs. I will take these to him. Thank you and goodbye.

*(The **COUNT** begins to push **LT. CRISIS** out the door when **JOYCE** enters from the kitchen, sees **LT. CRISIS** and does a quick turn around.)*

LT. CRISIS. You there!

COUNT. You two know each other?

JOYCE. Yes. Yes we do.

LT. CRISIS. How is everything at the lab?

JOYCE. Well…I…eliminated everything that shouldn't be there.

LT. CRISIS. The spray worked?

COUNT. Spray?

JOYCE. Yes. He told me there was a problem with my gas.

COUNT. That is a terrible thing to say!
LT. CRISIS. Well, why kill unnecessarily?
COUNT. I am shocked by your attitude!
JOYCE. It's all right, Count. I've learned to live with it.
LT. CRISIS. Well, she probably owns her own gas mask.
COUNT. You will leave my house immediately!
LT. CRISIS. I'm sorry...I didn't mean to...
COUNT. Goodnight!

*(The **COUNT** opens the door and **LT. CRISIS** walks out perplexed.)*

COUNT *(Continued)* I am sorry for that. We may have our differences but that was totally uncalled for.
JOYCE. Thank you, Count.

*(The **COUNT** closes the door. He looks at **JOYCE**, thinks for a moment and then opens the door a crack.)*

COUNT. It's, uh, warm tonight. I'll leave it open just a bit.
JOYCE. You know...this is a wonderful moment we've shared.
COUNT. Yes it is. Now get back to work.

*(**JOYCE** exits and the **COUNT** runs to the closet door letting **MRS. PUDDLEPONT** out.)*

MRS. PUDDLEPONT. How many mothballs do you keep in there? I feel faint.
COUNT. Everything is all right now...take a deep breath.

*(The **COLONEL** walks downstairs wearing one of the **COUNT**'s robes, admiring the material. The **COUNT** pushes **MRS. PUDDLEPONT** back in the closet and closes the door as she takes a deep breath.)*

COLONEL. Say...I like this.
COUNT. What...What are you doing?
COLONEL. Well I have to let my clothes dry.
COUNT. But...

*(**JOYCE** walks in from the kitchen sees the **COLONEL** and does a quick turn around.)*

COLONEL. You!

JOYCE. Hello.

COUNT. You two know each other?

COLONEL. Yes. And I thought we weren't going to be disturbed. What are you doing here anyway? Moonlighting?

JOYCE. I'm...straightening up the Count's books. They are a mess.

COLONEL. Is that true, Count?

COUNT. Supposedly, but I thought you were going to start with the tables.

JOYCE. But I can't finish the tables because the Count determined the figure I have presented to him was too large.

COUNT. Do not take it so personally.

JOYCE. I'll try not to. And just what are you doing here Colonel?

COLONEL. I was invited.

(He turns to leave.)

And don't worry. Before I left home I remembered to turn off the lights.

(The **COLONEL** *exits.)*

COUNT. Will you get back to work!

JOYCE. Ok, ok!

*(***JOYCE*** exits back into the kitchen. The* **COUNT** *is about to prop himself up with his arm against the door of the cellar, when* **MATTIE** *suddenly opens it from the other side. The* **COUNT** *falls through the opening, audibly THUMPING all the way down the steps. After a moments silence, His footsteps are heard reascending the stairway until at last He comes face to face with* **MATTIE***)*

MATTIE. *(Pause)* I missed you.

COUNT. I am a lucky duck.

MATTIE. How is everything going?

COUNT. Everything is going terribly! And why are you bothering me now!?

MATTIE. I wrote you a poem.

(She slips him a piece of paper)

COUNT. And just in the nick of time too.

*(The **COUNT** pushes **MATTIE** back into the cellar.)*

COUNT. What am I going to do?

*(The **COUNT** collapses on the couch and closes his eyes. **DR. GUNTER** quietly sneaks in through the window carrying a Doctor's bag and quietly approaches the **COUNT**.)*

DR. GUNTER. Tisk, tisk. Undt classical symptom of ze congenital insomniac. Vhat a dilemma. Do I remember mine medical oath to treat all patients? Or do I persist in mine desire to destroy him? Vait! As und Doctor, I can do both!

*(**DR. GUNTER** opens up his medical bag.)*

Insomnia is often associated mit a poor diet. Let us see if you can digest a steak...

*(He takes a large mallet and wooden stake out of his medical bag and positions it over the **COUNT**'s heart.)*

...While I cook your goose. Auf wiedersehen, Count.

*(**DR. GUNTER** begins whistling, "I've been working on the Railroad." He lifts the mallet up, and strikes the stake with it, driving it into the **COUNT**'s heart)*

COUNT. OUCH!

*(The **COUNT** sits up.)*

DR. GUNTER. Ouch? Vhat is zis ouch? You vill please die now. Vhy do you not die?

*(The **COUNT** removes the stake from his heart.)*

COUNT. Because my dear Wolfbaine, if you wish to kill a vampire the stake you drive into its heart must be made out of oak, and taken from a coffin that has lain in the Earth.

DR. GUNTER. Who wrote zat!? Some cheap attorney!?

COUNT. He wasn't cheap.

*(The **COUNT** takes the mallet from **DR. GUNTER** and hits him on the head with it. **DR. GUNTER** falls over, unconscious. The **COUNT** begins dragging **DR. GUNTER** by the legs frantically looking from some place to deposit him.)*

COUNT *(Continued. Muttering)* Modern architecture! Built in washers and dryers they have. But ask about built in burial vaults and they look at you like you are screwy. Well, who is screwy now?

*(As the **COUNT** drags **DR. GUNTER** behind a potted plant. The **COLONEL** walks downstairs wearing the **COUNT**'s robe.)*

COLONEL. Is she gone? You never told me how you thought I looked in your robe.

COUNT. I would prefer to see you in something with more frills. But if you do not wish…

COLONEL. I'll be right back!

*(The **COLONEL** runs back upstairs. The **COUNT** continues dragging **DR. GUNTER** across the room. As he passes the closet door it opens and **MRS. PUDDLEPONT** sticks her head through.)*

MRS. PUDDLEPONT. I can't breathe in here any longer!

COUNT. My breath has also been taken away, but by your beauty and poise and if you could just wait…

MRS. PUDDLEPONT. I'll wait!

*(**MRS. PUDDLEPONT** quickly shuts herself back in the closet. The **COUNT** continues dragging the **DR. GUNTER** across the room. As he passes the cellar door it opens a crack and **MATTIE** sticks her head through.)*

COUNT. Let me guess. You have painted a portrait of me?

*(**MATTIE** passes a portrait of the **COUNT** through the door.)*

MATTIE. Do you like it?

COUNT. It is lovely. And there are so many places I can hang a picture of myself riding a motorcycle naked. Yet, it needs something…Perhaps if you were sitting behind me…and *both* of us were wearing clothes, I should love it.

MATTIE. I'll be right back!

(MATTIE shuts herself back in the cellar. The COUNT begins dragging the DR. towards the front door.)

COUNT. I suppose under the porch is as good a place as any.

(The HEADLIGHTS of a car illuminate the window as it pulls up. The COUNT drags DR. GUNTER in the other direction.)

COUNT *(Continued)* I just knew I would be the one who would end up dusting the floor.

(The COUNT quickly sits DR. GUNTER in a chair at a small table with a chess board on it, and props the DR.'s head up by placing the DR.'s right hand under his chin, and then lifting his eyelids. The COUNT then moves a couple of pieces on the board and sits on the opposite side of the table. The doorbell rings).

COUNT. *(Softly and to himself)* Count Zescu, you are a genius!

(Loudly)

COME IN!

(MATTIE enters from the cellar door. MRS. PUDDLEPONT enters from the closet. The COLONEL enters from upstairs wearing a frilly robe and the LT. CRISIS. walks in through the front door. They stare at each other and gasp loudly.)

COUNT. Well now that wasn't right.

MRS. PUDDLEPONT. Mattie!

COLONEL. Lenora!

MATTIE. Uncle!

Scene 2

SETTING: *The main living room of the* **COUNT**'*s estate.*
AT RISE: *One hour later. It is still dark.*

DR. GUNTER, *the* **COLONEL**, **MRS. PUDDLEPONT**, *and* **LT. CRISIS** *are all strapped to gurneys with a medical tray positioned next to each.*

COLONEL. *(Softly)* Do you think he's mad that I didn't let him use the sock puppets?

LT. CRISIS. I think I hear him in the next room. Can you see him?

MRS. PUDDLEPONT. I think so. Is that an eggbeater he's holding?

COLONEL. Yes it is.

MRS. PUDDLEPONT. Funny. I don't see any eggs. Do you see any eggs where you are, John?

COLONEL. No. But don't panic. It is almost breakfast time and he does seem to be wearing an apron.

LT. CRISIS. I think that's a surgical gown, Colonel.

COLONEL. Really? Did somebody complain they weren't feeling well?

MRS. PUDDLEPONT. John, I think he's going to kill all of us!

COLONEL. What's your take, Lieutenant?

LT. CRISIS. I think I concur with your wife.

COLONEL. Hmm. Doctor?

DR. GUNTER. Yah, ze indications vould seem point to our certain demise.

COLONEL. Alright then. Lieutenant. I need a fall back position. What's our best hope?

LT. CRISIS. I say we go for a quick and painless death.

COLONEL. Excellent!

(Pause)

Wait a minute. The Count's or ours?

LT. CRISIS. Ours, Colonel.

COLONEL. A quick and painless death, eh? Any alternative?

LT. CRISIS. A slow and horribly painful death.

COLONEL. Not a lot of wiggle room there. Alright. Let me race those two around the track and see which one crosses the finish line first.

MRS. PUDDLEPONT. It's no use. The man is a monster!

LT. CRISIS. He's inhuman!

COLONEL. A fiend!

DR. GUNTER. Nice stainless steel gurneys, though. Ve could use a few, Colonel.

*(The **COUNT** enters, wearing a surgical gown and holding an eggbeater.)*

COUNT. Hello everyone. Comfortable?

COLONEL. You're off your rocker, Count. If this has anything to do with our using bats as experimental test subjects…

COUNT. It has everything to do with it.

COLONEL. But why? What can you do about it? It is the march of progress.

COUNT. I too have heard the march of progress. Through wood and hollow and mist covered valley the sounds of civilization have followed me. But these were unwelcome sounds. Their meaning was carried on the ends of flaming torches and on the points of wooden stakes. Those who remain, such as myself, do not regard this contest bitterly. Countless centuries before, a cruel fate had decreed we should exist as opponents. And I can promise you now that no act of charity or chivalry shall be made to mar the inevitable conclusion destiny has willed. Does that answer your question?

*(The **COLONEL** snores.)*

MRS. PUDDLEPONT. John!

COLONEL. Huh? Oh. Did he finish?

MRS. PUDDLEPONT. Yes, he finished. He's going to kill us!

COLONEL. Drat! Did he say how? Or is that another speech.

COUNT. I will not bore you any longer!

MRS. PUDDLEPONT. Oh no, Count. Please go on. I do so enjoy listening to you.

COUNT. You are very kind.

MRS. PUDDLEPONT. In fact I'd love to hear it again. You have such a mellifluous voice.

COUNT. You are not the first to say so. But…

MRS. PUDDLEPONT. And I'm sure the Colonel will pay attention this time. John…

COLONEL. Alright, alright.

COUNT. Well… I too have heard the march of progress. Through wood and hollow and mist covered valley the sounds of…

(The **COLONEL** *snores.)*

MRS. PUDDLEPONT. John!

COLONEL. Huh? Oh. What again?

COUNT. Enough! I have wasted too much time!

MRS. PUDDLEPONT. Maybe some coffee would…

COUNT. You expect me to brew your husband a pot of coffee so he can stay awake long enough for me to finish a speech telling him why I'm going to kill him. Isn't that asking a little too much?

COLONEL. It really is, dear.

COUNT. You are a very cool customer, Colonel.

COLONEL. I'm in the military, Count. The Lieutenant and I will gladly take the worst you can dish out.

*(**LT. CRISIS** raises his head and looks at the **COLONEL**.)*

COLONEL *(Continued)* But show a sense of decency and let my wife and Mattie go.

*(**DR. GUNTER** clears his throat.)*

COLONEL *(Continued)* Oh yes. And Dr. Gunter too. He's just a civilian. Dr. Gunter, you will conduct my wife and niece to safety.

DR. GUNTER. Vell, I vas vondering if I could stay behind to observe. Mit mine medical background I could insure appropriate operating room safety procedures are followed undt maintained.

(Everyone stares at **DR. GUNTER.***)*

DR. GUNTER. Vhat? What are you looking at? Don't tell me zat I am ze only von vondering vhat he is going to do mit ze eggbeater?

COUNT. No one is going anywhere. The experiment shall proceed.

COLONEL. I don't know what monstrous hold you have over my niece, but she'll never forgive you if anything happens to us.

*(***MATTIE*** walks in carrying a pie.)*

MATTIE. Fresh pie!

MRS. PUDDLEPONT. Mattie?! Don't you know this man is going to kill us?

MATTIE. I'm sorry, Auntie. Uncle. But I love him. And he promised me no one here would be killed.

COUNT. To be precise what I said was no one would be killed here. A semantical difference hardly worth discussing.

MATTIE. See Uncle. Everything is fine.

COUNT. You must leave now, Mattie. I do not have time for pie. I must get the drainage tubes.

MATTIE. Drainage tubes?

(The **COUNT** *exits.)*

COLONEL. Yes, Dear, drainage tubes! Even after twelve years in a progressive school you should still be able to figure that one out. Now quick! Untie us.

MATTIE. I can't. You'll try to kill him.

COLONEL. Gee, you think so?

MATTIE. But don't worry. This is not a regular pie.

(Whispering)

I made it out of garlic.

COLONEL. Sweetheart. If there is one thing I hate more than being operated on by a mad scientist, it's being operated on by a mad scientist with garlic on his breath.

MATTIE. You don't understand...

(The **COUNT** *enters.)*

COUNT. I cannot find them. Maybe it would be simpler just to drill some holes in the floor to catch the runoff...

COLONEL. Runoff, huh? Just what fiendish designs have you in mind for that eggbeater?

COUNT. Eggbeater? Oh. I thought it was a rib-spreader. Maybe I *should* wear my glasses more often.

MATTIE. *(To the* **COLONEL***)* See it was just an honest mistake. And you were worried.

COLONEL. Mattie, there will never be another one like you. But if your father tries to have another kid I hope they arrest him first.

MATTIE. *(Hugging the* **COLONEL***)* That's sweet!

COUNT. Enough with these domestic doings. Leave us now.

MATTIE. But you still haven't tasted my pie.

COUNT. I am not a pie person!

MATTIE. You don't like my poems...my paintings...

COUNT. Very well!

(The **COUNT** *eats a piece of the pie.)*

Happy? Now go away. And...and...and bring me a pillow.

(The **COUNT** *collapses.)*

COLONEL. Extraordinary thing! Mattie. I'm proud of you. I'm going to be a better uncle. After this is over you're coming to our house and we're going to eat and celebrate!

(He looks at the **COUNT** *on the floor.)*

Though I think we'll order out. Hurry now, and untie us.

MATTIE. No. I'm going to take the Count far away from here. I'll send someone over for you later.

(She looks at the **COUNT.***)*

Oh my. The Count doesn't look at all well.

DR. GUNTER. Silly little girl. You. Mit ze crush on ze Count. You have placed ze Count's life in extreme jeopardy mit your pie. Release me immediately undt I vill help.

*(***MATTIE** *looks confused and panicky. After a moments hesitation she releases* **DR. GUNTER.** *He goes over to the side of the* **COUNT,** *but picks up the papers the* **COUNT** *had dropped and reads them.)*

DR. GUNTER. Hmmm...

MATTIE. Hurry! Help him!

DR. GUNTER. Yah, yah. Hand me zat bottle.

*(***MATTIE** *hands Him a bottle and* **DR GUNTER** *pours out a small amount of the liquid into his handkerchief.)*

DR. GUNTER. Now, hold up ze Count's head.

*(***MATTIE** *holds up the* **COUNT***'s head.)*

MATTIE. Oh my precious darling! My special love! My sweet little paddycakes. My scrumptious umptious...

*(***DR. GUNTER** *quickly chloroforms* **MATTIE** *who quickly drops unconscious.)*

MRS. PUDDLEPONT. Oh my! John, look what he did? He chloroformed Mattie!

COLONEL. Well if he hadn't, I would have. She'd only be in the way right now.

*(***DR. GUNTER** *is intently reading the* **COUNT***'s papers.)*

COLONEL *(Continued)* Congratulations, Doctor. You're a hero.

DR. GUNTER. Zis paper is most interesting...

COLONEL. Well, time to unbuckle these straps.

DR. GUNTER. *(Still reading)* Most interesting indeed.

COLONEL. Right. Think you should be able to slice through these restraints with that scalpel on that table over there.

(**DR. GUNTER** *goes to the table but picks up a large pair of calipers instead and begins measuring the* **COLONEL**'s *cranium.*)

COLONEL *(Continued)* I don't mean to tell you your business, Doctor, but the scalpel is the sharp pointy thing with the silver blade.

(**DR. GUNTER** *looks at the calipers and refers to the papers he's holding as he slowly walks out of the room*).

COLONEL. Er, uh, Doctor…Oh Doctor…

MRS. PUDDLEPONT. What's he up to, John?

COLONEL. Well, let's see. My birthday's coming up. I might hazard a guess he's checking my hat size. You know these Germans. Have to be so damn precise about everything. Still, decent enough fellow for a sour kraut.

MRS. PUDDLEPONT. Darling…until he actually comes back with the hat, maybe it might be best not to upset him by referring to him as a sour kraut.

(**DR. GUNTER** *enters the room wearing a surgical gown.*)

COLONEL. You may have something there dear. Say Dr. Gunter. You're not planning to do what I think you're going to do?

(Pause)

Are you?

DR. GUNTER. I am.

COLONEL. Oh. Before you go any further, I must remind you that your citizenship test is coming up in a couple of weeks. This isn't going to look good.

MRS. PUDDLEPONT. Even if they grade on the curve you'll end up having to take the test at least twice.

DR. GUNTER. It is und chance I am villing to take.

LT. CRISIS. You'll never get away with this. Picture the entire U.S. Army bearing down on this place. And not one of them will be strapped helplessly to a gurney! Except Private Higgins, of course. Thinks he's a B-52 on fire. Been meaning to talk to you about him, Colonel. He's bringing down the morale of the pilots.

DR. GUNTER. Amazing. In your position you still have time to zink of others. Such Courage! Such a fine physical specimen! Yah. You vill be ze first.

COLONEL. Hang on, son. Or should I say…Captain?

LT. CRISIS. You mean you're promoting me?

COLONEL. It's the very least I can do.

DR. GUNTER. Ze least you can do is make him a Major.

COLONEL. A Major!? Are you crazy!?

(Pause)

Look who I'm asking.

LT. CRISIS. He's right, Doctor. A field promotion to Captain is a great honor.

COLONEL. There. See. He's happy.

DR. GUNTER. Poppycock! Think of ze ordeal he is about to undergo!

COLONEL. *(Loud whisper to* **DR. GUNTER***)* Oak clusters don't grow on trees!

DR. GUNTER. *(Loud whisper to the* **COLONEL***)* Vhat? It is coming out of your pocket?

COLONEL. *(Loud whisper to* **DR. GUNTER***)* That's not the point! It took me 14 years…

MRS. PUDDLEPONT. John…

COLONEL. Ok, ok. Congratulations, Major.

DR. GUNTER. Excellent! Remember Mrs. Puddlepont, you are a vitness.

*(****DR. GUNTER*** *wheels the Major out of the room.)*

MRS. PUDDLEPONT. That poor boy!

COLONEL. Wonder why the Doctor was interested that I'd

promote him.

MRS. PUDDLEPONT. And I wonder why it took you so long!

COLONEL. Look. I feel for the lad as much as you. But there's an inspector from the GAO office already making my life hell. True, we may never get out of this. But if we do and she sees me starting to hand out promotions like candy cigarettes she'll be on me like a peahen on a june bug.

(**JOYCE** *walks in*)

What did I tell you!

MRS. PUDDLEPONT. Help us!

(**JOYCE** *starts to unstrap them.*)

MRS. PUDDLEPONT. *(Continued)* Oh Thank God! Who are you?

COLONEL. She's the inspector from the GAO office.

JOYCE. No. I'm Joyce Lyonhartt, from the Herald Tribune.

COLONEL. A reporter!? You mean you lied to me!?

MRS. PUDDLEPONT. Oh, What's the difference?

COLONEL. I'll tell you the difference! I've been filling out requisitions by candlelight!

(He jumps off the gurney.)

Drinking prune juice instead of orange juice for breakfast! Eating left over Spam! And driving 10 miles an hour to save fuel! You try driving to the office at only 10 miles an hour after you've just had a meal of Spam and prune juice!

MRS. PUDDLEPONT. Who cares!? We've got to save the Lieutenant.

COLONEL. That's Major. Which isn't minor. He almost outranks me now.

MRS. PUDDLEPONT. Save him!

COLONEL. Right. I'll go get the Doctor. You see to Mattie and tie up the count. But don't hurt him. When I come back he's going to be all mine!

(BLACKOUT)

End of Act II Scene II

Scene 3

SETTING: Living room of the **COUNT***'s estate.*

AT RISE: One hour later. It is still dark. The **COUNT** *is sitting down with a cold compress on his forehead.* **DR. GUNTER** *is also sitting down while the* **COLONEL** *stands over him holding a gun.* **MRS. PUDDLEPONT** *stands next to him.* **MATTIE** *is lying unconscious on the couch.* **JOYCE** *is at a desk reading some documents. And* **LT. CRISIS** *is covered in bandages sitting in a chair.*

MRS. PUDDLEPONT. It took you two hours to find him!?

COLONEL. It's a large house. There were no doors marked, "Quiet, Mad Doctor at Work." I'm sure he understands. Right lad?

(The **COLONEL** *slaps him on the back and he moans loudly)*

COLONEL *(Continued)* Sorry, son. I wish we could be sure of what the Doctor did to him. Do you remember anything? Anything at all?

*(***LT. CRISIS** *motions the* **COLONEL** *to come closer and whispers in his ear.)*

COLONEL. I see. It's worse than I thought.

MRS. PUDDLEPONT. What is it?

COLONEL. He remembers I promoted him.

MRS. PUDDLEPONT. Just make sure you don't forget.

COLONEL. I'm a man of my word. And the Captain knows it.

MRS. PUDDLEPONT. Major!

(He takes his wife aside)

COLONEL. Major? For what? Lying on his back for two hours?

MRS. PUDDLEPONT. Look at him!

COLONEL. He's fine. A few small cuts here and there. Why I've seen more nicks on a basketball court in Madison

Square garden.

*(The **COLONEL** waves cheerily to **LT. CRISIS**. **LT. CRISIS** makes a pathetic attempt to wave back. As he extends his arm, he falls out of the chair and onto the floor)*

COLONEL *(Continued)* Alright. He's a Major again. But I don't think he's going to thank either of us when every time he enters a room someone says, "A Major Crisis has arrived."

*(**MRS. PUDDLEPONT** and the **COLONEL** put **LT. CRISIS** back in the chair. **MATTIE** walks over to **LT. CRISIS**.)*

MATTIE. You look awful. How do you feel?

LT. CRISIS. You're the most beautiful woman I think I've ever seen.

COLONEL. Easy son. Let me get some extra bandages for your jaw.

LT. CRISIS. My jaw's fine Colonel.

COLONEL. Really? Try talking that way again to my seventeen year old niece and see.

MRS. PUDDLEPONT. Never mind, John. Let's be grateful that at least it's over.

JOYCE. It isn't over yet.

*(**JOYCE** is holding some documents by her side and looking out the window, as the faint sound of bats can be heard outside.)*

MRS. PUDDLEPONT. What do you mean?

JOYCE. Doctor Wolfbaine Gunter is in reality Doctor Wolfbaine Bunter – escaped war criminal.

COLONEL. No!

JOYCE. Yes. By changing the first letter of his last name he was able to avoid detection by our intelligence forces for the past 10 years.

DR. GUNTER. Yah, zat ended up working out a lot better than I vould have thought.

JOYCE. But that wasn't his only trick.

(**JOYCE** *goes up to* **DR. GUNTER** *and removes his glasses, which are attached to a big nose and mustache. Underneath,* **DR. GUNTER** *is still is wearing a pair of glasses and a big nose, but no mustache.*)

COLONEL. Ingenious!

MRS. PUDDLEPONT. I can't believe it! A war criminal! And he used our bathroom once!

JOYCE. And it wasn't the first time he had been relieved. He was broken in rank by the German High Command for trying to genetically create an exact twin of Hitler.

DR. GUNTER. Big deal! Everyone undt his brother vas trying to pull off zat one! Zey just got mad because I vas programming mine Hitler lose to me in poker.

(Pause)

Plus I zink, zey didn't like ze fact that I gave him und nice set of breasts. It vas late undt I vas feeling silly... you know.

JOYCE. And as for Count Zescu, Colonel...you have captured yourself a real live vampire.

COLONEL. Vampire!? You mean like, Dracula?

COUNT. *(Wringing out the cold compress)* Dracula!? Please! He is the only vampire with a press agent. Father will not even let him come over to the house anymore. Is there any more cold water?

MRS. PUDDLEPONT. But if there ever were such a creature as Dracula, surely he must be dead.

COUNT. It is not so easy a thing, to kill a vampire. Though some of us seem to keep trying awfully hard. Garlic pie!

MATTIE. I told you I was sorry.

COUNT. I am not talking to you.

COLONEL. Well fine. With that garlic still in him he won't be much trouble. We'll just pack the two of them up and drive off.

COUNT. Really? I believe you will find that the bats outside have bitten through the valve stems of all the tires.

MRS. PUDDLEPONT. All those bats…and I hear wolves… Waiting for us…We can't go outside.

JOYCE. But can we stay inside? Locked inside a house with a man who underwent a surgical procedure which may have turned him into a threat to every living thing around him.

COLONEL. The Major? Nonsense!

JOYCE. I can't understand all the writing in these papers. But there doesn't seem to be much doubt about a drawing of a man exploding, and killing everyone around him with the words, "Kaput Americana!", written in blood.

DR. GUNTER. Vas I doodling again?

COLONEL. You mean, there is a bomb inside the Major?! But who would be crazy enough to devise such a surgical procedure?

COUNT. You were, Colonel. The bats. Remember? I merely refined the idea and hoped to place the bomb where it would do the most good. How does it feel now?

COLONEL. So, putting the shoe on the other foot. Is that it?

*(The **COUNT** looks at his shoes quizzically)*

COLONEL *(Continued)* But you, Doctor…The war is over!

DR. GUNTER. War is never over. Zey are just interrupted by inconvenient periods of peace. Or pieces, as you vill soon see.

MRS. PUDDLEPONT. About to be destroyed by your own experiment. It's almost as if there was a lesson in that.

COLONEL. We can talk about that later, dear. Hmmm? Hmmm?

JOYCE. But the bomb can't be primed to go off yet. It would accomplish nothing.

COLONEL. Mattie, take care of the Major. Don't let him move around too much.

*(**MATTIE** gives **LT. CRISIS** a glass, which he drinks out of slowly.)*

COLONEL *(Continued)* I wonder how the bomb is armed?

JOYCE. *(Reading the documents)* Hard to say. Apparently a capsule inside him somewhere reacts to the presence of C2H2OH. Whatever that is. Minutes later, after the capsule has completely dissolved a chemical reaction occurs which...detonates the Major.

COLONEL. I can't help but think it has something to do with the Doctor wanting me to promote him to Major instead of Captain.

JOYCE. What's the difference between a Captain and a Major?

COLONEL. Major is a command rank. More money and prestige. Preceded by a quiet celebration at the Officers Club. Everybody gathers around. Lots of partying, eating, drinking...

JOYCE. Drinking! C2H2OH! That's the chemical symbol for alcohol!

*(**LT. CRISIS** spits out the drink.)*

COLONEL. Mattie! What did you give the Major to drink?

MATTIE. Water.

COLONEL. Good.

MATTIE. Ice.

COLONEL. Uh-oh.

MATTIE. And bourbon.

COUNT. That's my girl.

COLONEL. Major. Listen to me. How much did you drink?

*(The **MAJOR** hiccups.)*

DR. GUNTER. Ze Major is armed undt dangerous. Nothing can be done. You have but a few minutes left to live.

COLONEL. Then stop it!

DR. GUNTER. Impossible! Zis entire house und everyone inside vill be destroyed! Ha-ha! Ha-ha-ha! Ha-ha-ha-ha-ha!

JOYCE. But you'll be killed too.

DR. GUNTER. *(Pause)* I knew zat.

LT. CRISIS. There's something that Dr. Bunter has failed to take note of.

(**LT. CRISIS** *struggles to his feet. The* **COUNT** *begins to observe with growing interest.*)

LT. CRISIS. *(Continued)* Those choices are always available. I choose to go outside alone to avoid endangering the rest of you.

COLONEL. Wait. That is very commendable, Major. But everything that has happened is ultimately my responsibility. And I won't let you suffer the consequences alone. I'm going with you. Who knows? Maybe there's something I can do.

MRS. PUDDLEPONT. Wait. If you're going, John so am I.

COLONEL. No! You have too much yet to live for.

MRS. PUDDLEPONT. I couldn't live in a world without you, John. Don't worry. It will be quick I'm sure. And we will be in each other's arms.

JOYCE. Wait. I'm the one who's actually responsible. I knew all along the danger to everyone. But I ignored it. All I wanted was a good story. If it's to be written in blood, it's only right it should be written with mine also.

COLONEL. No. You're young, with your whole life in front of you.

JOYCE. The choice isn't yours. I'm coming.

COLONEL. I'm sorry for everything I ever said to you.

MATTIE. Wait. I'm coming too. And don't try to stop me, Uncle.

COLONEL. Fine.

MRS. PUDDLEPONT. John!

COLONEL. I mean, uh, no. You have your whole life ahead of you…Etcetera…Etcetera…Etcetera.

MATTIE. But if I hadn't fallen in love with the Count, none of this would have ever happened.

COLONEL. She's got a point there.

MRS. PUDDLEPONT. John…

COLONEL. I mean, no dear. You must stay behind.

MATTIE. If you force me to stay behind I'll just kill myself anyway. I want to die with my family.

COLONEL. All right then. Come with us child.

COUNT. Wait. I am the one who is responsible. In trying to teach you a lesson I have become the same as those I have found fault with. I wish to be with you when the bomb explodes.

COLONEL. Big deal! The bomb isn't going to hurt him.

MATTIE. Uncle!

COUNT. He is right. But the sun will rise any moment, and my end shall come soon enough. Anyway, the bomb wouldn't exactly have felt like a Swedish massage either you know.

*(The **COUNT** puts his arm around the **COLONEL**.)*

COUNT *(Continued)* But now, I wish to be with people who taught me that people who don't eat people are some of the luckiest people of all.

COLONEL. That's beautiful.

(To his wife)

If he starts singing, I'm going to detonate the Major myself.

MATTIE. Please my beloved...wear my locket as a promise of our love ever lasting.

*(**MATTIE** removes the locket from around her neck. As she fastens it around the **COUNT**'s neck, the front of his shirt rolls up like a window shade.)*

COUNT. Can we go now?

*(They all exit, leaving **DR. GUNTER** alone, looking perplexed. After a moment, **DR. GUNTER** gets up and walks down into the basement. The front door opens and the **COLONEL**, **MRS. PUDDLEPONT**, **JOYCE**, **MATTIE** and the **COUNT** re-enter.)*

COLONEL. Of course, we really wouldn't be accomplishing anything.

MRS. PUDDLEPONT. Yes, I think we already made our point.
JOYCE. No sense in being melodramatic.
MATTIE. You have to learn to live with tragedy.
COUNT. I am sure the Major understands.
LT. CRISIS. Maybe the bomb won't even go off...

(As **LT. CRISIS** *limps towards the front door the* **COUNT** *closes it without looking, leaving the* **MAJOR** *outside)*

COUNT. We can all learn a lot from such a brave man.
COLONEL. Nothing to do but wait I guess.

(THEY all sit down)

MRS. PUDDLEPONT. *(Pause)* It was nice at least to see the Major rise so quickly in rank. Oh. You know what I mean.
JOYCE. *(Pause)* He'll leave his mark everywhere. Oh. You know what I mean.
COUNT. *(Pause)* He was a great guy.
COLONEL. *(Angry)* I'm afraid I don't know what you mean by that!
JOYCE. Wait a minute. Where's Dr. Bunter?
MRS. PUDDLEPONT. That's right. Where is he? He's the guilty one.
JOYCE. He must still be in the house. All right everyone. Let's search it fast.
COLONEL. Let's do it for the Major. The bravest man who ever lived. But first, could someone look out the window and make sure the Major isn't standing by any of our cars.

(Everyone exits through a different door. **DR. GUNTER** *enters slowly through the basement door)*

DR. GUNTER. Everyone gone. I am all alone. No way out. Mit so many experiments schtill to be performed.

*(***DR. GUNTER** *picks up a scalpel and lies down on a gurney, strapping himself down and positioning a mirror above him.* **DR. GUNTER** *softly sings to the tune of, "Me and My Shadow")*

DR. GUNTER. *(Continued)* Just me, undt mine scalpel. Valking down ze Avenue. Just me, undt mine scalpel. Feeling old and oh so blue.

(**DR. GUNTER** *begins cutting into himself*)

DR. GUNTER. *(Continued)* Oh zat smarts! Und now ladies und gentlemen. Doctors und esteemed colleagues. Ouch! Observe now as I attempt to rearrange certain vital organs inside ze thorax cavity. Ze squeamish may vish to step outside. Ouch! Ahhhhh! Oooooo! Eeeeeee! Ouch! Ekkk! Ouch! Ouch! Eeeeee! Ha-Ha-Ha-Ha! Sorry. Zat vas my funny bone I just hit. EeeeeeAhhh-hOoooooo! Oops. Zat one vasn't.

(Barely able to speak)

At least I can die vit ze satisfaction zat mine experiment on ze Major vas...an...unmitigated...success.

(**LT. CRISIS** *runs into the house.*)

LT. CRISIS. Look everybody! I'm fine! I got so nervous I threw up the capsule!

DR. GUNTER. You threw up ze capsule!

LT. CRISIS. Dr. Bunter! What...what have you done to yourself!?

DR. GUNTER. Don't cry, Seymour. It is all right.

LT. CRISIS. It's Herbert. And you are the last person I would cry over. But why...

DR. GUNTER. It vas all over anyway. I knew zey were getting closer to discovering who I really vas. Mine life has come to a close. Give...give me your hand to hold. Vhat? Oh. Let me guess. You are still mad at me.

LT. CRISIS. Mad at you?! I think you are the most insane, inhuman monster I have ever met and I won't have anything to do with you anymore!

DR. GUNTER. Zat is what my wife said when we first met. But before long she agreed to marry me undt I agreed to release her from ze decompression chamber. So you see Archibald, zese things have a way of working themselves out.

LT. CRISIS. You forced your wife to marry you by placing her in a decompression chamber?!

DR. GUNTER. Vell, I vas never very good mit poetry und besides, I saved a bundle on flowers. Help me, und maybe I vill give you ze keys to ze chamber for you undt zat special girl.

LT. CRISIS. No!

DR. GUNTER. You don't like girls?

LT. CRISIS. I like girls' fine! But not like you! You're right, doctor. Your time has come to an end. You are heartless. You should have never been born. I wish I could... I wish I could...

DR. GUNTER. Kill me yourself? I believe you do not need to bother.

LT. CRISIS. Then you know you're not going to make it. Is there a message you want me to deliver to anyone?

DR. GUNTER. Just ask everyone not to think to unkindly about me. It is asking a lot I know, Herbert. But you must!

*(**DR. GUNTER** grabs at **LT. CRISIS**, tearing part of his surgical dressing off, and it drops to the floor. **LT. CRISIS** pulls back.)*

LT. CRISIS. It's not Herbert, it's..! Oh wait. It is Herbert. That's the first time you ever got my name right.

DR. GUNTER. Really? Ve are finally friends. Please now... Close mine eyelids...I do not have ze strength...

LT. CRISIS. All right. Wait a minute. What are you holding in your hand?

DR. GUNTER. *(Pause)* Nothing.

LT. CRISIS. Dr. Bunter...

DR. GUNTER. Ok, ok!

*(**DR. GUNTERR** throws down a surgical power saw.)*

DR. GUNTER. *(Continued)* Nothing personal. Just never tried von of zese models before.

(DR. GUNTERR *turns his head and lies still.* LT. CRISIS *is about to close* DR. GUNTER*'s eyelids, but thinks a moment, and carefully pulls a sheet over him instead.* LT. CRISIS *stands back. Suddenly there is a LOUD EXPLOSION and FLASH outside, forcing the windows open.* LT. CRISIS *quickly exits to investigate.* JOYCE *enters, sees part of a Band-Aid on the floor and picks it up.*)

JOYCE. Oh my! Blown clean through the window.

(*The* **COLONEL**, **MRS. PUDDLEPONT**, **MATTIE** *and the* **COUNT** *enter.*)

COUNT. I heard the explosion. It must be over.

MRS. PUDDLEPONT. The poor Major.

MATTIE. It's horrible.

COLONEL. And it's all my fault!

(*Taking the Band-Aid from* **JOYCE.**)

Thank you.

(*The* **COLONEL** *takes the Band-Aid that* **JOYCE** *is holding and loudly blows his nose into it.*)

JOYCE. Colonel, that's all that's left of the Major!

(*The* **COLONEL** *looks inside the Band-Aid.*)

COLONEL. Oh, sorry son. That will rinse right out.

(*The* **COLONEL** *reverently places the Band-Aid on a table and steps back and salutes. The rest form a semicircle and quietly bow their heads.* **LT. CRISIS** *enters, sees everyone standing quietly and joins them.*)

LT. CRISIS. *(Pause)* What are we doing?

COLONEL. We're honoring a fine and noble...

(*The* **COLONEL** *pauses, then slowly turns to face the* **LT. CRISIS.**)

COLONEL *(Continued)* You're alright!?

(*Everyone is happily relieved.* **LT. CRISIS** *walks over to the table and picks up the Band-Aid.*)

LT. CRISIS. Oh! You thought...Well, I'm flattered by the tribute. Touched really. Deeply moved knowing how you all really feel about me...

(**LT. CRISIS** *looks at the Band-Aid closely, stops, does a double-take, is about to say something but the* **COLONEL** *quickly takes the Band-Aid out of the* **LT. CRISIS***'s hand.*)

COLONEL. But the explosion Major. We heard an explosion.

LT. CRISIS. It wasn't me. I threw up the capsule. But your car, Colonel. Apparently one of the bats back at the base got loose, saw Dr. Bunter's World War II helmet in your car and...

COLONEL. My new Crown Victoria?

(**LT. CRISIS** *hands the* **COLONEL** *the hood ornament.*)

LT. CRISIS. I'm sorry. The doctor didn't fare much better.

(**LT. CRISIS** *pulls back a sheet on a gurney revealing* **DR. GUNTER** *and everyone gasps.*)

MRS. PUDDLEPONT. Oh my! What happened to him?

LT. CRISIS. He finally ran out of experimental subjects... Until only he was left.

(*The* **COUNT** *runs his finger across* **DR GUNTER***'s body and tastes his blood.*)

COUNT. He was a very bitter man.

COLONEL. (*Melodramatically*) I did not witness what happened, I only thank God my wife and I were spared.

MRS. PUDDLEPONT. (*Hugging the Colonel*) Oh John...

COLONEL. No, no. I'm just rehearsing what to tell the insurance company about our car. They'll never believe a bat blew it up.

COUNT. Tell them, in the days following World War II, the United States Army began an experimental project it was hoped would change the course of modern warfare.

(*The* **COUNT** *dramatically walks over to the window and stands by it.*)

COUNT *(Continued)* Tell them, it was a fool's errand, for it matters not how you change the implements of warfare if man himself remains unchanged. Tell them of the Major.

*(The **COUNT** stands on the window ledge and spreads his cape.)*

And that the power to demand human flesh can not survive or compete with the instinct to surrender it freely, nobly and selflessly. Tell them of the Major's example you witnessed here tonight. For it is the only hope that mankind has, if mankind is to have any hope at all.

COLONEL. If you don't mind, I think I'll just say I left the keys in the car in a bad neighborhood.

COUNT. As you wish. Farewell, Mattie. You shall live forever as the better part of me.

*(The **COUNT** flaps his arm and jumps off the ledge and lands on the ground.)*

Rotten garlic! I, uh…I, uh, felt like walking anyway. Goodbye.

MATTIE. Watch out for the…

*(As the **COUNT** takes a step the handle of a rake snaps up and the hits the **COUNT** in the face.)*

MATTIE *(Continued)* …Rake.

*(The **COUNT** picks up the rake and hurls it off the porch, and stares at **MATTIE**, who just looks down at the floor.)*

COLONEL. We can't let him get away! Quick, after him!

COUNT. Foolish mortal! Even in my weakened state do you believe you are any match for me!?

*(The **COUNT** takes a step and accidentally puts his foot in a pail which he struggles to remove, and falls through the window back into the house.)*

COLONEL. All right everybody, jump him!

(MATTIE interposes herself between the COUNT and the COLONEL.)

MATTIE. No! Don't you see? What the Count was talking about. It was like his Valentine. Not just to me. But to the whole human race.

COLONEL. That's fine dear.

(To his wife)

Lenora, can we purchase chloroform in six packs?

MRS. PUDDLEPONT. John, perhaps we should let him go. What has he really done, anyway?

COLONEL. But he's a vampire!

(The COUNT finally pulls the pail off his foot and hurls it to the floor.)

COUNT. Yes, and your puny attempts to capture me will be of no avail!

(The COUNT turns dramatically to leave but catches the corner of his cape on a hook on the wall and is held fast.)

Oh, for cryin' out…

MATTIE. I'm sorry, Uncle. If you hurt him you'll have to hurt me too! I'm running away with him. To the farthest reaches of the Earth!

(MATTIE removes the COUNT's cape from the hook and helps him out of the window, but knocks his head against the sill.)

MRS. PUDDLEPONT. Mattie no! John, do something!

COLONEL. *(Pause)* Don't forget to write.

MRS. PUDDLEPONT. John… !

COLONEL. For heaven's sake, dear, she's practically a grown woman.

COUNT. Now just a minute…

(MATTIE drags the COUNT by the arm.)

COLONEL. Bye son.

MATTIE. Come my beloved.

COUNT. Really now! Just who is the most feared and menacing creature around here anyway?!

COLONEL. You'll see.

(MATTIE drags the COUNT out of view.)

MRS. PUDDLEPONT. How could you let that happen?

COLONEL. Really dear, we weren't much older when we ran away together. And things worked out fine for us. And you know…You haven't changed a bit since we first met.

MRS. PUDDLEPONT. Neither have you John…except for that negligee I saw you wearing earlier.

COLONEL. Oh that little subterfuge. I was attempting to smoke out the Count with the classic military maneuver known as the Malaysian Mantrap. Basic tactics you pick up at West Point.

LT. CRISIS. Gee, Colonel, that doesn't ring any bells…

COLONEL. If you want to hear bells ring maybe you'd like to man the front desk at the supply hut…In Guam. Which I can arrange if you interrupt me again.

LT. CRISIS. Sorry.

(The COLONEL and MRS. PUDDLEPONT gently help LT. CRISIS up and slowly lead him out the front door.)

COLONEL. So there I was. Mano-a-mano. Armed with nothing more than a pair of razor sharp stiletto high heels…

(The COLONEL and MRS. PUDDLEPONT and LT. CRISIS exit. JOYCE turns on her tape recorder and speaks into it.)

JOYCE. Final dispatch from Heatstroke, California. The case proving the existence of vampires has disappeared into the mist filled night, leaving me without any creditable evidence to place before a disbelieving public.

(She walks center stage.)

But for any of you whose doubts may slowly give way

when walking alone late at night under a pale blue moon I give you a warning. If you hear the sudden fluttering of wings and the air being torn behind you by the swift descent of something large and ominous, listen carefully.

(SHE walks to the front of the stage not seeing the **COUNT.** *cross by the window to pick up HIS wallet)*

If that is followed by the sound of something crashing into garbage cans, and then tripping over its own two big feet as it lets out a string of unprintable Rumanian curses, heed it well. For Count Zescu is back. A gold plated, blue ribbon klutz of a Vampire if ever there was one. Who would have trouble staying aloft if he was strapped to a rocket.

(The **COUNT** *sticks HIS head through the window)*

COUNT. I heard that! And for your information…

(The **COUNT** *trips and disappears from view as thunder and lightening strike)*

COUNT. *(From offstage)* Never mind.

(BLACKOUT)

End of Play

PROPERTY PLOT

PRESET

Act I, Scene 1

Sewing kit (desk drawer)
Small rubber ball (on floor in corner)
Flower in vase (on table)
Diary (in purse on table)

Act I, Scene 2

Dinner table having:
    Gravy boat
    Bowl of grapes
    Vase of flowers
    Dinner plates and settings

Act I, Scene 3

Small box with insects (on table)
A few small wire cages with bats inside (on stand)
Glass and pitcher of water (on desk)
Globe (on desk)
Box (on floor next to desk) containing:
    German army helmet
    Lugar
    Letter in envelope

Act II, Scene 1

Perfume (in purse on desk)
Large book (on desk)
Portrait of Count (inside hall closet)
Decanter and glasses (on table)
Phonograph (on stand)
Chess set (on small table)

Act II, Scene 2

Surgical tray (on stand) holding following:
    Bottle of chloroform and cotton strips
    Scalpel
    Calipers
Large well thumbed though manuscript (on table)

Act II, Scene 3

Papers (on desk)
Pitcher of water and glass (on table)
Decanter of liquor (on table)
Scalpel (in desk)
Surgical saw (beneath gurney)
Rake (outside window)
Pail (outside window)
Wallet (outside window)

PROP TABLE

Feather duster (Joyce)
Flask (Joyce)
Large spider (Count)
Valentine card (Mattie)
Wolf's paw (Count)
Small model fighter plane (Colonel)
Pad and pencil (Joyce)
Fumigation canister (Joyce)
Bar of soap (Gunter)
Several daggers (Gunter)
Forty-five-caliber service revolver (Lieutenant)
Papers (Colonel)
Petunia (Count)
Small portable tape recorder (Joyce)
Meat hooks (Count)
Plate of éclairs (Colonel)
Bottle of wine (Colonel)
Phonograph record (Mrs. Puddlepont)
Papers (Lieutenant)
Piece of paper (Mattie)
Medical bag containing one mallet and stake (Gunter)
Egg Beater (Count)
Pie (Mattie)
Locket (Mattie)
Hood ornament (Lieutenant)

COSTUME PLOT

COUNT ZESCU: Formal black evening dress with tails. Winged collar on white shirt. White vest and bow tie. Somewhat fancy medallion worn around neck with red ribbon. Red sash and black cape with red lining. Hair slicked down. Shoes shined to high polish.

MATTIE: Poodle skirt and tight sweater. Black and white saddle shoes with white socks. Hair done in pony tail. Later, sexy evening robe and slippers. Hair free about shoulders.

JOYCE LYONHARTT: Simple gray utility dress a housekeeper might wear with over sized wrinkled sweater, flats, and hair somewhat unkempt. Later, inexpensive business suit or dress. Hair neatly arranged. Later still, utility overalls with workers hat with front bill. Boots scuffed. Lastly, an attractive stylish very smart skirt and blouse combo. Blouse billowy and silky and skirt with slit up side. High heels.

COLONEL PUDDLEPONT: 50's style khaki army uniform with appropriate insignia. Later, a see-through ladies night gown with khaki underclothing underneath.

LIEUTENANT CRISIS: 50'S style khaki army uniform with appropriate insignia. Later, bandages covering almost entire torso.

MRS. LENORE PUDDLEPONT: Sensible dress with basic print. Later, provocative evening dress showing much more bosom.

DR. GUNTER: An old fashioned white medical smock with buttons down the side of his neck, chest and his side. Wears a pair of Jackboots. Wire frame glasses. Mustache.

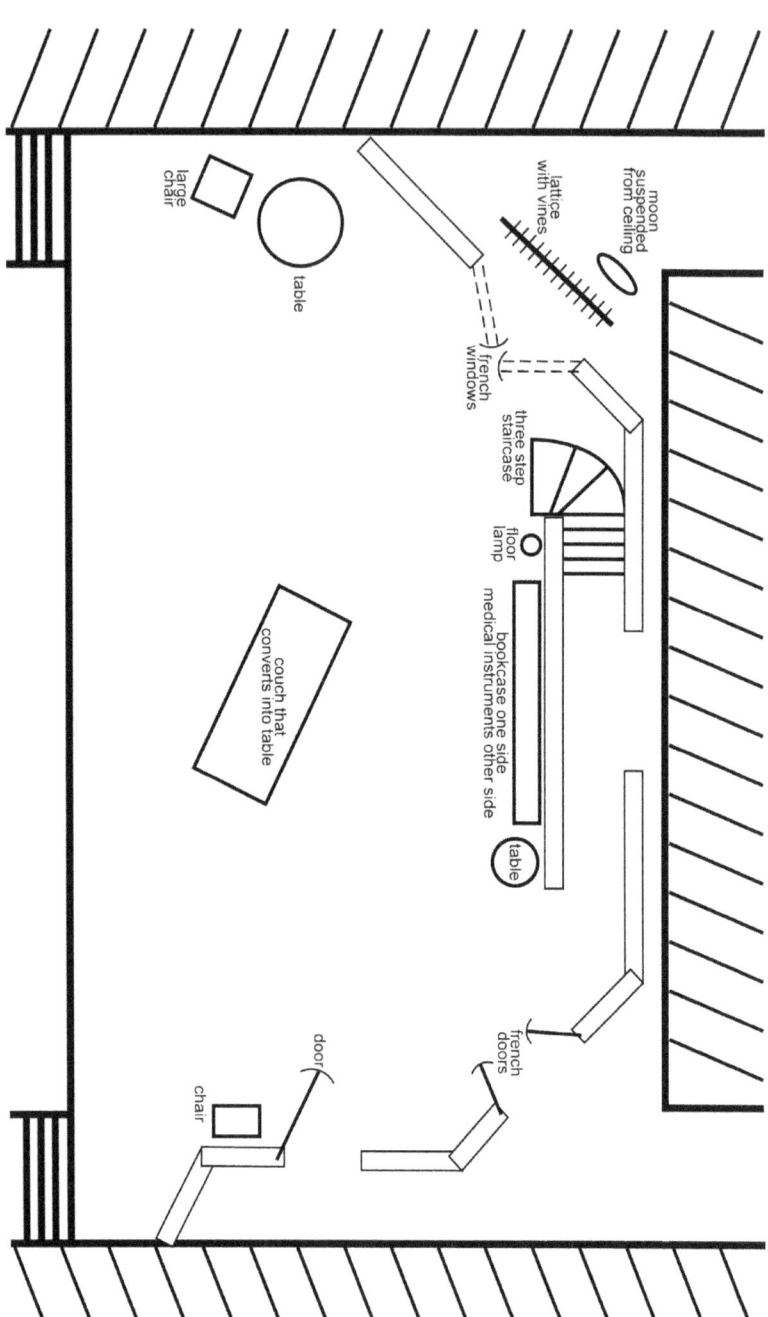

From the Reviews of
A VAMPIRE REFLECTS...

"The cast, under Vaughn Armstrong's energetic, campy direction, has a ball with the nonsense, not only because it provides the kind of over-the-top theatrics every actor would kill for but because of the dialogue's Preston Sturges-like locomotion and the story's underlying spoof of Cold War attitudes.

The real fun is the rat-a-tat-tat talk and punning and sympathizing for an obscure Count who complains that 'Dracula just had a better press agent'.

One of the funnier touches in a script that relentlessly dishes out the one-liners is introducing a real ghoul who makes the Count look like a pushover: Dr. Gunter (Miguel Marcott). He is the prototypical ex-Nazi now in the U.S. government's employ but whose real agenda is to terrorize the base."
- Los Angeles Times

Also by
Frank Semerano...

Kaputnik

Murder Me Once

Next Stop Murder

The Tangled Snarl

Thataway Jack

Please visit our website **samuelfrench.com** for complete descriptions and licensing information

OTHER TITLES AVAILABLE FROM SAMUEL FRENCH

GUTENBERG! THE MUSICAL!
Scott Brown and Anthony King

2m / Musical Comedy

In this two-man musical spoof, a pair of aspiring playwrights perform a backers' audition for their new project - a big, splashy musical about printing press inventor Johann Gutenberg. With an unending supply of enthusiasm, Bud and Doug sing all the songs and play all the parts in their crass historical epic, with the hope that one of the producers in attendance will give them a Broadway contract – fulfilling their ill-advised dreams.

"A smashing success!"
- *The New York Times*

"Brilliantly realized and side-splitting!
- *New York Magazine*

"There are lots of genuine laughs in *Gutenberg!*"
- *New York Post*

SAMUELFRENCH.COM

www.ingramcontent.com/pod-product-compliance
Lightning Source LLC
Chambersburg PA
CBHW050514020526
44111CB00052B/2287